The Synoptic Gospels and Source Criticism

The Synoptic Gospels and Source Criticism

under the supervision of
Richard P. Thompson

Theological Essentials

Library of Congress Cataloging-in-Publication Data

Richard P. Thompson (creator).
The Synoptic Gospels and Source Criticism / Richard P. Thompson
140 + x pp. cm. 12.7 x 20.32
ISBN 979-8-89731-288-7 (Print)
ISBN 979-8-89731-254-2 (Ebook)
ISBN 979-8-89731-256-6 (Kindle)
ISBN 979-8-89731-260-3 (Abridged Audio Discussion)

1. Bible. Gospels—Sources.
2. Synoptic problem.

BS2555.2 .T46 2026

This book is available in other languages at www.DTLPress.com

Cover Image: The Four Gospels from the Book of Kells
https://en.wikipedia.org/wiki/Saint_symbolism#/media/File:KellsFol027v4Evang.jpg

Contents

Series Preface

Artificial Intelligence (AI) is changing everything, including theological scholarship and education. This series, *Theological Essentials*, is designed to bring the creative potential of AI to the field of theological education. In the traditional model, a scholar with both mastery of the scholarly discourse and a record of successful classroom teaching would spend several months—or even several years—writing, revising and rewriting an introductory text which would then be transferred to a publisher who also invested months or years in production processes. Even though the end product was typically quite predictable, this slow and expensive process caused the prices of textbooks to balloon. As a result, students in developed nations paid more than they should have for the books and students in developing nations typically had no access to these (cost-prohibitive) textbooks until they appeared as discards and donations decades later. In previous generations, the need for quality assurance—in the form of content generation, expert review, copy-editing and printing time—may have made this slow, expensive and exclusionary approach inevitable. However, AI is changing everything.

This series is very different; it is created by AI. The cover of each volume identifies the work as "created under the supervision of" an expert in the field. However, that person is not an author in the traditional sense. The creator of each volume has been trained by the DTL staff in the use of AI and *the creator has used AI to create, edit, revise and recreate the text that you see*. With that creation process clearly identified, let me explain the goals of this series.

Our Goals:

Credibility: Although AI has made—and continues to make—huge strides over the last few years, no unsupervised AI can create a truly reliable or fully credible college or seminary level text. The limitations of AI generated content sometimes originates from the limitations of the content itself (the training set may be inadequate), but more often, user dissatisfaction with AI-generated content arises from human errors associated with poor prompt engineering. The DTL Press has sought to overcome both of these problems by hiring established scholars with widely recognized expertise to create books within their areas of expertise and by training those scholars and experts in AI prompt engineering. To be clear, the scholar whose name appears on the cover of this work has created this volume—generating, reading, regenerating, rereading and revising the work. Even though the work was generated (in varying degrees) by AI, the names of our scholarly creators appear on the cover as a guarantee that the content is equally credible with any introductory work which that scholar/creator would pen using the traditional model.

Stability: AI is generative, meaning that the response to each prompt is uniquely generated for that specific request. No two AI-generated responses are precisely the same. The inevitable variability of AI responses presents a significant pedagogical challenge for professors and students who wish to begin their discussions and analysis on the basis of a shared set of ideas. Educational institutions need stable texts in order to prevent pedagogical chaos. These books provide that stable text from which to teach, discuss and engage ideas.

Affordability: The DTL Press is committed to the idea that affordability should not be a barrier to knowledge. *All persons are equally deserving of the right to know and to understand.* Therefore, ebook versions of all DTL Press books are available from the DTL libraries without charge, and available as print books for a nominal fee. Our scholar/creators are to be thanked for their willingness to forego traditional royalty arrangements. (Our creators are compensated for their generative work, but they do not receive royalties in the traditional sense.)

Accessibility: The DTL Press would like to make high quality, low cost introductory textbooks available to everyone, everywhere in the world. The books in this series are immediately made available in multiple languages. The DTL Press will create translations in other languages upon request. Translations are, of course, generated by AI.

Our Acknowledged Limitations:

Some readers are undoubtedly thinking, "but AI can only produce derivative scholarship; AI can't create original, innovative scholarship." That criticism is, of course, largely accurate. AI is largely limited to aggregating, organizing and repackaging pre-existing ideas (although sometimes in ways that can be used to accelerate and refine the production of original scholarship). Still while acknowledging this inherent limitation of AI, the DTL Press would offer two comments: (1) Introductory texts are seldom meant to be truly ground breaking in their originality and (2) the DTL Press has other series dedicated to publishing original scholarship with traditional authorship.

Our Invitation:

The DTL Press would like to fundamentally reshape academic publishing in the theological world to make scholarship more accessible and more affordable in two ways. First, we would like to generate introductory texts in all areas of theological discourse, so that no one is ever forced to "buy a textbook" in any language. It is our vision for professors anywhere to be able to use one book, two books or an entire set of books in this series as the *introductory* textbooks for their classes. Second, we would also like to publish traditionally authored scholarly monographs for Open Access (free) distribution for an advanced scholarly readership.

Finally, the DTL Press is non-confessional and will publish works in any area of religious studies. Traditionally authored books are peer-reviewed; AI-generated introductory book creation is open to anyone with the required expertise to supervise content generation in that area of discourse. If you share the DTL Press's commitment to credibility, affordability and accessibility, contact us about changing the world of theological publishing by contributing to this series or a more traditionally authored series.

With high expectations,
Thomas E. Phillips
DTL Press Executive Director
www.thedtl.org
www.DTLpress.com

Introduction

This book, *The Synoptic Gospels and Source Criticism,* introduces one of the most important areas of New Testament study: the literary relationships among Matthew, Mark, and Luke. These three Gospels share much in common, often telling the same stories in similar words, yet they also diverge in significant ways. How these Gospels are related to one another, who wrote first, who borrowed from whom, and whether there were other sources now lost, has been a central question for generations of scholars. This question, often labeled the Synoptic Problem, lies at the heart of source criticism, the discipline concerned with identifying the sources that underlie biblical texts.

The chapters that follow guide readers through the history, theories, and consequences of source-critical study of the Synoptic Gospels. The book begins by setting out the emergence of the problem in early modern scholarship and then explores the major hypotheses that have shaped discussion: Markan priority, the Two-Source Theory, the Farrer Hypothesis, the Griesbach proposal, and the Augustinian tradition. Subsequent chapters test these hypotheses through worked examples and extended case studies, highlighting how they attempt to explain agreements and divergences in the texts. The study then considers the theological and interpretive consequences of these models, as well as the new horizons opened by digital tools, memory studies, and global perspectives.

This book is written to be academically rigorous yet accessible to a wide range of readers. It is intended for those who wish to understand how source-critical issues shape interpretation of the Synoptic Gospels, whether they approach the text as students, pastors, teachers, or general readers. The aim has been to present material that is both informative and engaging: academically grounded, yet attentive to the needs of those seeking to understand why these questions matter for the study of Scripture and for theology.

The Synoptic Gospels and Source Criticism does not offer a final solution to the questions it raises, for the field itself resists closure. Rather, it provides a map of the major hypotheses, the evidence marshaled in their support, and the implications they carry for exegesis, theology, and faith. To study the Synoptic Gospels through the lens of source criticism is to see more clearly how these texts were shaped, how they speak in both harmony and dissonance, and how their plurality continues to enrich the life of the Church. If this book helps readers to read the Synoptics with sharper eyes and greater appreciation for their complexity, it will have achieved its purpose.

Part I
Foundations

Chapter 1
The Synoptic Gospels and the Meaning of Source Criticism

The Synoptic Gospels

The first three Gospels in the New Testament, Matthew, Mark, and Luke, have been called the Synoptic Gospels since the eighteenth century, when scholars began to notice the peculiar way in which they can be "seen together" (from the Greek *syn,* "together," and *opsis,* "view"). When these texts are placed side by side, whether in printed parallels or in modern digital alignment tools, their literary relationship becomes immediately apparent. They narrate many of the same events in Jesus' ministry, often in the same order and with remarkably similar wording in Greek. This overlap is sometimes so close that it cannot be explained by oral tradition alone. Sentences and even whole paragraphs appear virtually identical across two or three of the Gospels.

Yet at the same time, differences abound. The Synoptics diverge in vocabulary, alter the order of episodes, and adapt details of a story to suit their distinctive emphases. For example, Matthew presents Jesus as a new Moses, arranging his teaching into five great discourses. Luke situates Jesus within a sweeping history of Israel and the nations, structuring the ministry as a journey toward Jerusalem. Mark, by contrast, prefers a brisk style, vivid but rough, with less polished Greek and abrupt transitions. These similarities and differences together create what scholars call the Synoptic Problem: how can we best explain the literary relationship between these three Gospels? The discipline of source criticism is the method that addresses that question.

What Is Source Criticism?

Source criticism studies the literary relationships among the Synoptic Gospels, seeking to identify the sources that the evangelists used in writing their accounts. It asks whether one Gospel writer had access to another's work, whether they drew upon common written sources now lost, or whether oral tradition accounts for their similarities.

The word "criticism" should not be misunderstood. In modern usage it often suggests disapproval or negativity. In this context, however, it means careful analysis and discernment. To engage in source criticism is to compare texts closely, to trace patterns of agreement and divergence, and to construct models that best account for the evidence. The goal is not only to resolve an academic puzzle but to understand the nature of the Gospels themselves: how they came to be, how the story of Jesus was transmitted, and how early Christian communities preserved and shaped tradition.

Source Criticism in Relation to Other Methods

It is important to situate source criticism within the broader landscape of biblical study. Textual criticism examines the thousands of manuscript copies of the New Testament, identifying variants introduced by scribes and working to reconstruct the earliest attainable text. Form criticism moves further back, focusing on the small units of tradition, such as parables, miracle stories, and pronouncement saying that circulated orally before being written down. Redaction criticism looks at how each evangelist edited and arranged material, highlighting theological emphases: Matthew's interest in the fulfillment of Scripture, Luke's concern for the marginalized, and Mark's stark portrayal of discipleship.

Source criticism, by contrast, investigates the relationship between the written Gospels themselves. It is a more basic inquiry than form or redaction criticism because it asks what sources each evangelist may have had before him. Only once this relationship is clarified can one ask how oral tradition shaped the sources (form criticism) or how the evangelists edited them (redaction criticism). Source criticism therefore provides the foundation for much of modern New Testament scholarship.

Why Source Criticism Matters

At first glance, source criticism might appear to be a technical exercise, a question of literary dependence with little consequence for interpretation. In fact, the implications are profound. If Mark was the earliest Gospel, as many argue, then Mark's portrait of Jesus (which is urgent, apocalyptic, and less embellished) may be closest to the first narrative retelling of his life and ministry. If Matthew or Luke wrote first, then the shape of early Gospel tradition looks very different, with major consequences for how readers reconstruct the earliest Christian preaching.

The question of sources also affects how one understands the figure of Jesus. If a sayings source, commonly called Q (from the German word *Quelle*, "source"), once existed, then one of the earliest documents about Jesus contained little or no narrative of his life but rather a collection of his teachings. This would suggest that the first generation of Christians treasured Jesus above all as a teacher of wisdom and a prophet of God's reign. By contrast, if Luke simply used Matthew, then Q disappears, and the figure of Jesus emerges from a literary dialogue between evangelists rather than from a lost early document. Each hypothesis carries weighty implications for theology, history, and the authority of tradition.

The Evidence for Source Criticism

Source critics marshal several lines of evidence. Agreement in wording and order is the most obvious. When Matthew, Mark, and Luke recount the same story using identical or nearly identical Greek, it is highly unlikely that they did so independently. Shared order across episodes strengthens the case for literary dependence.

The "triple tradition" refers to stories found in all three Synoptics, such as the feeding of the five thousand or the passion narrative. These passages reveal both the closeness of the parallels and the subtle variations that must be explained by any hypothesis. The "double tradition" (which is material found in Matthew and Luke but absent from Mark) raises even sharper questions. How did Matthew and Luke come to share the Beatitudes, the Lord's Prayer, and the mission discourse, if not from a common source? Was that source written, as the Q hypothesis suggests, or did Luke simply copy Matthew, as the Farrer hypothesis argues?

Other kinds of evidence are also significant. Editorial seams reveal how one evangelist joined material together, often betraying reliance on a prior text. Stylistic tendencies show each writer's fingerprints: Luke's fondness for polished Greek and Septuagintal diction, Matthew's formulaic citations of Scripture, Mark's penchant for vivid detail and parataxis ("and… and… and…"). Phenomena such as "editorial fatigue," when a writer begins to alter a source but inadvertently lapses back into its wording, further strengthen arguments for literary dependence. Each of these clues must be weighed carefully, for no single piece of evidence can decide the matter alone.

Early Efforts and Key Figures

While early Christian writers such as Papias and Augustine commented on the order and origins of the Gospels, the modern study of their literary relationships emerged in the

Enlightenment. The publication of parallel synopses was crucial. Johann Jakob Griesbach's *Synopsis* (1776) made it possible to see the Gospels side by side, providing an indispensable tool for systematic comparison.

Theories soon followed. Johann Gottfried Eichhorn proposed an *Urevangelium,* a lost "original Gospel" from which Matthew, Mark, and Luke all drew. Christian Hermann Weisse (1838) offered a new solution: Mark was written first, and Matthew and Luke independently drew from Mark as well as a sayings source, later called Q. Heinrich Holtzmann (1863) refined this into what became known as the Two-Source Hypothesis, which, with modifications, became the dominant model of the twentieth century.

The most influential synthesis came from B. H. Streeter in *The Four Gospels* (1924). Streeter defended Markan priority and Q, but also added two additional sources, M and L, to account for material unique to Matthew and Luke. He even proposed a hypothetical Proto-Luke, an early form of Luke's Gospel consisting of Q and L material prior to Mark's influence. Streeter's "Four-Document Hypothesis" became the classic statement of source criticism for a generation.

Later scholars introduced refinements and challenges. John S. Kloppenborg argued that Q itself shows various compositional layer: sapiential teachings first, later expanded with prophetic and apocalyptic material. Others, such as Mark Goodacre, have argued that Q never existed, advocating instead that Luke used Matthew directly. Meanwhile, defenders of the Griesbach (Two-Gospel) Hypothesis, such as William R. Farmer, and of the Augustinian Hypothesis, such as John Wenham, have kept alternative solutions alive. The conversation remains vigorous, and the Synoptic Problem continues to be one of the most debated questions in New Testament studies.

What Is at Stake

The study of sources is not merely a historical curiosity. It shapes how readers approach the authority and diversity of the Gospel witness. If the evangelists used each other's works, then they were not passive collectors of tradition but creative theologians, shaping the material for new contexts. If lost sources such as Q existed, then those sources themselves have theological significance, even if they no longer survive. If oral tradition played a greater role than we sometimes allow, then memory, performance, and community identity emerge as key factors in preserving Jesus' story.

For modern readers, source criticism is an invitation to deeper engagement with the Gospels. It uncovers the artistry and theological intention behind each evangelist's work. It challenges simplistic harmonization by honoring both similarities and differences. Above all, it reminds us that plurality lies at the heart of the Christian Gospel tradition: three distinct voices telling the story of Jesus in ways both convergent and diverse, each shaped by sources, tradition, and theological insight.

Chapter 2
The Synoptic Data Set

Introducing the Synoptic Data

The investigation of the Synoptic Problem begins not with theory but with description. The Gospels themselves present a body of data that demands explanation. Matthew, Mark, and Luke are not three independent stories of Jesus' life; they are deeply interrelated works. Their relationship is visible in the structure of their narratives, in the wording of their stories, and in the theological emphases they choose to highlight. Source criticism is the method by which scholars attempt to account for these relationships, but the first step is to describe them carefully.

From the eighteenth century onward, scholars recognized that the best way to observe the data was to place the Gospels side by side. A *synopsis* presents parallel passages in columns, allowing readers to see agreements and differences at a glance. Johann Jakob Griesbach's *Synopsis* (1776) was a groundbreaking tool, followed in later centuries by ever more refined editions, culminating in Kurt Aland's *Synopsis Quattuor Evangeliorum,* which remains the scholarly standard today. In recent decades, digital resources have expanded the possibilities of synoptic study. Bible software can calculate percentages of verbal overlap, and searchable databases allow rapid identification of unique vocabulary. The format may change, but the basic task remains the same: to scrutinize the texts and let their patterns emerge.

Triple Tradition

The term *triple tradition* refers to material that appears in all three Synoptic Gospels. The most striking examples include major episodes such as the Baptism of Jesus, the Feeding of the Five Thousand, the Confession of Peter, the Entry into Jerusalem, and the Passion Narrative. In these passages one can often see a clear backbone running through Mark, with Matthew and Luke reproducing Mark's account while adapting it in their own ways.

For instance, in Mark's healing of Jairus's daughter (Mk 5:21–43), the story is vivid and dramatic. The father is named, the girl's age is specified, the crowd presses around Jesus, and the Aramaic phrase *Talitha koum* ("Little girl, get up") is preserved. When Matthew tells the story (Mt 9:18–26), nearly all of this detail disappears; the father is unnamed, the girl is already dead when he approaches Jesus, and the narrative is condensed to a bare outline. Luke (8:40–56) preserves Mark's vivid details but smooths out the grammar and refines the storytelling. In this one example we see the three evangelists in conversation: Mark providing raw material, Matthew abbreviating, and Luke polishing. If Mark was first, the literary logic is clear. If Matthew or Luke came first, Mark's role becomes much harder to explain.

The triple tradition provides the most obvious evidence of interdependence, but it also contains puzzles. At times Matthew and Luke agree against Mark, inserting small phrases or omitting details in the same way. These "minor agreements" will become crucial in later debates. For now, it is enough to recognize that the triple tradition is the backbone of the Synoptic comparison and the arena in which arguments about priority are most forcefully tested.

Double Tradition

The *double tradition* refers to material found in Matthew and Luke but absent from Mark. Here we meet many of the teachings most often associated with Jesus: the Beatitudes, the Lord's Prayer, the Temptation Narrative, the Mission Discourse, and the Parable of the Lost Sheep. The similarity in wording between Matthew and Luke is often close enough to suggest a common written source, yet the differences in arrangement are striking.

Matthew tends to collect sayings into large, carefully structured discourses. The Sermon on the Mount (Mt 5–7) gathers beatitudes, ethical teachings, and the Lord's Prayer into a single climactic speech. Luke, by contrast, scatters the material: some appears in the Sermon on the Plain (Lk 6:20–49), some in the travel narrative (Lk 9–19), some in isolated settings. Why do Matthew and Luke share so much in common yet arrange it so differently?

This question lies at the heart of the Synoptic Problem. Those who defend the Two-Source Hypothesis argue that Matthew and Luke drew independently on a common written sayings source, known as Q. The differences in arrangement, on this view, reflect the freedom of each evangelist to order material according to theological aims. Advocates of the Farrer Hypothesis, however, counter that no hypothetical Q is necessary: Luke simply drew upon Matthew, borrowing his sayings but redistributing them to suit his own narrative plan. The double tradition thus becomes a litmus test for one's solution to the

Synoptic Problem
Special Material in M and L

Beyond the triple and double traditions, each Synoptic Gospel contains material that is unique. Scholars label this content M (unique to Matthew) and L (unique to Luke). These categories do not necessarily refer to specific written sources; rather, they serve as shorthand for traditions that only one evangelist preserves.

M material includes the genealogy of Jesus (Mt 1:1–17), the visit of the Magi (2:1–12), and parables such as the Wheat and the Tares (13:24–30) and the Sheep and the Goats (25:31–46). These passages underline Matthew's interest in Jesus as the fulfillment of Scripture and as a teacher who redefines righteousness for the community.

L material includes some of the most beloved parables in the New Testament: the Good Samaritan (10:29–37), the Prodigal Son (15:11–32), and the Rich Man and Lazarus (16:19–31). It also includes uniquely Lukan narratives such as the story of Zacchaeus (19:1–10) and the Emmaus Road appearance (24:13–35). These passages reveal Luke's theological priorities: the inclusion of outsiders, the joy of repentance, and the conviction that the risen Christ continues to guide his community.

B. H. Streeter (1924) argued that M and L were themselves written sources, though no such documents survive. Other scholars prefer to regard them as oral traditions known to Matthew and Luke. Either way, they demonstrate the breadth of early Christian tradition: not all that the evangelists recorded was shared in common.

Tools for Analyzing the Data

The careful description of Synoptic relationships was advanced by the work of scholars such as John C. Hawkins, whose *Horae Synopticae* (1899) remains a classic. Hawkins catalogued patterns of agreement and divergence, compiled word statistics, and demonstrated systematically what earlier scholars had noticed: Mark's language is rougher and more primitive, while Matthew and Luke often refine or expand upon it.

Later handbooks, such as Robert H. Stein's *Studying the Synoptic Gospels* (1987) and E. P. Sanders and Margaret Davies's volume of the same name (1989), built upon this foundation, offering clear criteria for recognizing dependence: agreement in wording, agreement in order, the presence of editorial seams, and the cumulative weight of stylistic tendencies. Modern digital tools now allow scholars to test these criteria with even greater precision, but the fundamental questions remain the same.

The task is to describe the data honestly, without letting theory predetermine observation. Any hypothesis, whether Two-Source, Farrer, Griesbach, or Augustinian, must be tested against this body of evidence. If it cannot explain the distribution of material across triple tradition, double tradition, and special sources, it cannot stand.

Why the Data Matters

The classification of Synoptic material may appear dry, but it is the essential ground on which all later arguments rest. Without a careful account of what Matthew, Mark, and Luke share, and where they diverge, theories become speculative. The data disciplines the imagination, ensuring that hypotheses remain accountable to the text.

More profoundly, the Synoptic data testify to the richness of the Gospel tradition. They show that early Christians told the story of Jesus in ways both consistent and diverse. Some material was shared widely, shaping the core narrative of Jesus' life and death. Other material was preserved in local traditions, remembered differently in different communities. The triple, double, and special traditions together remind us that there was never a single way to tell the story of Jesus. Diversity was present from the beginning, woven into the very fabric of the tradition.

Source criticism, therefore, is not only about solving a literary puzzle. It is also about appreciating the complexity of early Christian memory. The Synoptic Data Set is our window into that world: a world where tradition was transmitted, adapted, and cherished, and where three evangelists, working with overlapping sources, created the distinct works that continue to shape Christian faith and scholarship today.

Chapter 3
Historical Survey

Framing the Question Across the Centuries

The Synoptic Problem did not emerge fully formed in modern times. Reflections on Gospel order, authorship, and relationship run from the earliest Christian centuries to the present. What has changed is not the basic puzzle, the coexistence of similarity and difference, but the tools and assumptions used to approach it. This chapter traces the conversation from patristic witnesses through Enlightenment experimentation, nineteenth-century consolidation, and twentieth- and twenty-first-century refinement. Along the way, it introduces voices whose arguments have shaped how readers understand the origins of Matthew, Mark, and Luke.

Patristic Witnesses

Memory, Authority, and Order

Early Christian writers commented on the Gospels in the language of memory and authority rather than modern literary theory. Papias of Hierapolis, writing in the early second century, claimed that Mark wrote down Peter's recollections "not in order," while Matthew composed the "sayings" in "Hebrew." These remarks are tantalizing but opaque. They testify that recollection and translation mattered to early

Christians, yet they do not map neatly onto modern hypotheses. Irenaeus affirmed the fourfold Gospel as the church's providential inheritance, and Origen recognized differences among the accounts. In the Latin West, Augustine proposed the sequence Matthew, then Mark, then Luke in *De Consensu Evangelistarum,* arguing that Mark abbreviated Matthew and that Luke wrote with knowledge of both. For centuries this Augustinian hypothesis provided the default framework, not because it was tested against Greek synopses, but because it cohered with ecclesial memory and apologetic need.

From Harmonies to Synopses
The Birth of Comparison

Medieval and early modern readers often negotiated difference by producing Gospel harmonies, which are continuous narratives that blended the four accounts into one. These works were useful for devotion and preaching but had the unfortunate side effect of masking divergence. The decisive turn came when scholars began to place the Gospels side by side. Johann Jakob Griesbach's *Synopsis* (1776) was revolutionary because it made agreements and differences visible at a glance. What harmonies concealed, the synopsis revealed: repeated phrases, shared sequences, and competing arrangements. The synopsis did not solve the problem, but it created the laboratory in which modern source criticism could work.

Enlightenment Experimentation
Lost Originals and New Sequences

The eighteenth century produced bold proposals that treated the Gospels as historical-literary artifacts. Johann Gottfried Eichhorn advanced the idea of an *Urevangelium,* a lost "original Gospel" from which the Synoptics descended. Others suggested families of earlier documents or stages of translation. Meanwhile, Griesbach articulated what would later be called the Two-Gospel Hypothesis: Matthew first, Luke used Matthew, and Mark conflated or abbreviated the two. The Enlightenment's essential move was methodological. It freed investigation from purely traditional sequences and invited testable explanation of textual phenomena. Though many early schemes were short-lived, they opened conceptual space for later models.

Nineteenth-Century Consolidation
Markan Priority and the Two-Source Idea

In the nineteenth century, close comparison in Greek and advances in textual criticism reshaped the conversation. Karl Lachmann argued (1835) that Mark's sequence underlies the other two, a claim grounded in observable order rather than ecclesial tradition. Christian Hermann Weisse (1838) combined Markan priority with a second written source, later called Q, to account for material common to Matthew and Luke but absent from Mark. Heinrich Holtzmann (1863) systematized this Two-Source Hypothesis, and it gained adherents because it seemed to explain more data with fewer ad hoc moves than its rivals. Meanwhile, the critical edition of the Greek New Testament by Westcott and Hort (1881) gave scholars a more reliable textual base for comparison, and John C. Hawkins's *Horae Synopticae* (1899) quantified stylistic tendencies that earlier generations had only sensed.

The Streeter Synthesis and the Four-Document Hypothesis

The early twentieth century saw a comprehensive statement in B. H. Streeter's *The Four Gospels* (1924). Streeter defended Markan priority and Q but also proposed distinct sources M (special Matthew) and L (special Luke), and even a Proto-Luke composed of Q and L material onto which Markan passages were later added. This Four-Document Hypothesis became the classic account for much of the century, not because it ended debate but because it offered a coherent map: Mark explains the backbone of shared narrative, Q accounts for shared sayings, and M and L explain special material. Streeter's synthesis influenced generations of introductions, commentaries, and classrooms.

Alternative Lines

Griesbach Revived and Q Rejected

Consensus invited counterproposal. In the mid-twentieth century, Austin Farrer argued that scholars could dispense with Q if they allowed that Luke used Matthew directly. Building on this, Michael Goulder and later Mark Goodacre developed the Farrer (No-Q) Hypothesis, sharpening tools such as editorial fatigue to detect direct dependence. In parallel, William R. Farmer revived the Griesbach or Two-Gospel Hypothesis, with Bernard Orchard and Harold Riley defending Mark as a conflator of Matthew and Luke. These alternatives forced Two-Source advocates to refine their claims, particularly regarding the distribution of double-tradition material and the status of the so-called minor agreements of Matthew and Luke against Mark, catalogued extensively by Frans Neirynck.

Late Twentieth and Twenty-First Centuries Layers, Memory, and Canon

By the late twentieth century, debates no longer turned only on whether Q existed but also on what kind of document it might have been. John S. Kloppenborg argued for stratification within Q, with sapiential material at its core and prophetic-apocalyptic layers added later. James D. G. Dunn emphasized oral tradition and the dynamics of living memory, cautioning against overly literary solutions. Francis Watson, with a canonical perspective, reframed the question by highlighting the theological significance of the fourfold Gospel as a deliberate reception of diverse witnesses. Digital tools multiplied: stylometry, corpus linguistics, and searchable databases enabled more granular tests of wording, order, and style, even as interpreters recognized the limits of quantification for historical judgments.

What Changed and What Did Not

Across these centuries, both the evidential base and the standards of argument evolved. Early appeals to tradition gave way to comparison of Greek texts; harmonies yielded to synopses; impressionistic judgments were supplemented by statistics; literary models were checked against patterns of order, wording, and redactional seams. Yet the heart of the matter remained constant. Readers sought a simple, comprehensive, and noncircular explanation for why the Synoptic Gospels look the way they do. No single hypothesis commands universal assent because the evidence is complex and the phenomena admit multiple, partially overlapping explanations. Each family of solutions (i.e., Two-Source, Farrer, Griesbach, Augustinian) illuminates some features while leaving others unresolved.

Primary Sources and Reference Tools

Modern inquiry relies on a set of tools and reference works that crystallize this history. Griesbach's *Synopsis* initiated the parallel-column method; Aland's *Synopsis Quattuor Evangeliorum* provides the standard modern reference. The Westcott–Hort edition and subsequent critical texts supply the base for comparison. Hawkins's statistics, Stein's methodological criteria, and Sanders and Davies's handbook model responsible use of evidence. Collections on minor agreements, studies of editorial fatigue, and reconstructions and critiques of Q (from Streeter to Kloppenborg) offer contrasting lenses through which the same data can be viewed.

Conclusion
A Tradition of Debate

The historical survey shows that source criticism is best understood as a tradition of debate rather than a single settled answer. Patristic voices preserved memories of authors and order. Enlightenment scholars taught readers to test claims against the text. Nineteenth-century critics established methods and models still in use. Twentieth-century figures synthesized, revised, and resisted, while contemporary scholars have added new dimensions of memory studies, canon, and digital analysis. The chapters that follow will not erase disagreement but will equip readers to recognize its lineage, evaluate its arguments, and participate in a conversation that is as old as the church and as current as today's research.

Part II
Major Hypotheses

Chapter 4
Markan Priority

The Significance of the Question

At the heart of the Synoptic Problem lies one of the simplest yet most consequential questions in New Testament study: which Gospel came first? If Mark wrote first, then Matthew and Luke depended upon him, adapting his narrative for their own theological and pastoral purposes. If Mark wrote last, then he condensed and edited material from his predecessors. The answer determines not only how we reconstruct the literary history of the Gospels but also how we understand the development of early Christian tradition and theology.

The theory of Markan priority (i.e., that Mark's Gospel was the earliest and that Matthew and Luke each used Mark as a principal written source) has become the cornerstone of modern source criticism. Its importance reaches far beyond literary curiosity. It shapes how scholars interpret the growth of early Christian proclamation, the formation of Gospel genres, and even the figure of Jesus as remembered in the earliest narrative tradition.

Evidence from Narrative Order

The most striking feature of the Synoptic parallels is the consistency of narrative order.

Across long stretches of the Galilean ministry, the Passion narrative, and the journey to Jerusalem, Matthew and Luke follow Mark's sequence of events even when they differ in wording or in the amount of detail included. Where Matthew and Luke diverge in order, they typically each preserve Mark's sequence rather than agreeing with one another against him.

This pattern is best explained if Mark provided the basic narrative outline upon which Matthew and Luke built. They could add, expand, or relocate individual stories, but they rarely dismantled the structure inherited from Mark. The opposite scenario (that Mark abbreviate and rearrange two longer predecessors) is considerably harder to sustain. It would require Mark to eliminate large sections of Matthew and Luke while somehow maintaining the same sequence they shared. The simplest explanation of the data is that Mark's order came first.

Evidence from Wording and Detail

In the triple-tradition material, where all three Synoptics recount the same story, the wording of Matthew and Luke often agrees verbatim with Mark. The amount of verbal overlap is too great to be explained by coincidence or oral tradition. Mark's wording frequently stands at the base of both Matthew and Luke's versions, while each of them makes small stylistic improvements or theological clarifications.

Consider the healing of Jairus's daughter (Mk 5:21–43; Mt 9:18–26; Lk 8:40–56). Mark tells the story with vivid, almost cinematic detail. He names Jairus, includes the interruption of the woman with the hemorrhage, and preserves the Aramaic command *Talitha koum*. Matthew's version shortens the episode drastically: the girl is already dead when the father approaches, and most of the descriptive color disappears. Luke retains Mark's structure but refines the Greek style and heightens the sense of awe. Such patterns are repeated throughout the triple tradition. Mark's form is longer, rougher, and more primitive; Matthew and Luke's are polished expansions.

Brevity, Primitivity, and Style

Mark's Gospel is the shortest of the three, yet it contains the most vivid narrative detail. He is fond of the historical present ("and he says," "and they come"), employs frequent parataxis ("and… and… and…"), and often retains Aramaic expressions or Semitic syntax. His Greek is energetic but unpolished, his transitions abrupt, his narrative pace urgent.

Matthew and Luke, by contrast, tend to smooth Mark's rough edges. They convert colloquial expressions into formal Greek, remove redundancies, and sometimes soften portrayals of the disciples' misunderstanding. Matthew often expands Mark by adding teaching material and explicit references to Scripture; Luke reshapes Mark's sequence into a carefully structured journey narrative that begins in Galilee and moves resolutely toward Jerusalem. These tendencies (i.e., both Mark's rough primitivity and the later evangelists' refinement) support the view that Mark stands earliest. It is far easier to imagine Matthew and Luke improving Mark's style than to imagine Mark systematically degrading the literary quality of two polished sources.

Theological Development and Narrative Expansion

If Mark wrote first, then the theological development evident in Matthew and Luke follows naturally. Mark's Gospel emphasizes secrecy, conflict, and suffering. Jesus is the misunderstood Son of God whose messiahship is revealed only through the cross. Matthew and Luke, using Mark, expand this story into broader theological vistas.

Matthew presents Jesus as the new Moses, fulfilling Scripture and providing authoritative teaching for the church. His five great discourses transform Mark's scattered sayings into organized instruction. Luke, in turn, reinterprets Mark through the lens of salvation history: God's purposes unfold from Israel to the nations, and the Spirit drives the narrative from Galilee to Jerusalem and then, in Acts, from Jerusalem to the ends of the earth. Markan priority therefore undergirds redaction criticism, for only when Mark stands first can Matthew's and Luke's distinctive theological editing be recognized as such.

Editorial Seams and the Markan "Sandwich"

Mark's narrative style reveals traces of composition that later evangelists adjust or eliminate. He frequently connects episodes with formulaic transitions such as "and immediately," "and again," "and he began to teach," which function as seams joining material from different sources. These seams often remain visible in Matthew and Luke but are smoothed or relocated.

A particularly distinctive feature of Mark is intercalation, or the "Markan sandwich." He begins a story, interrupts it with another, and then returns to complete the first. The healing of Jairus's daughter, interrupted by the woman's healing, is the best-known example. Matthew collapses the two healings into a single streamlined narrative; Luke preserves both but reorders the detail. These patterns point to Mark as the base text from which others worked.

Counterarguments and Alternative Views

Opponents of Markan priority raise several classic objections. The first concerns the phenomenon of minor agreements, where Matthew and Luke occasionally agree against Mark within triple-tradition material. These agreements, though numerous, are typically minor: shared omissions, small additions, or harmonizing changes. Some suggest they imply direct contact between Matthew and Luke. Advocates of Markan priority reply that many can be explained by textual transmission or natural editorial tendencies that two writers could independently make when adapting Mark.

Another objection is that Mark lacks certain major elements found in Matthew and Luke: infancy narratives, the Sermon on the Mount, and the Lord's Prayer. If Mark wrote first, why would he omit these treasures? The answer lies in Mark's purpose. His Gospel is a passion narrative with an extended introduction; it focuses on Jesus' deeds and the revelation of his identity through suffering rather than on extended teaching. The absence of these materials fits his aim rather than contradicting it.

A further objection claims that Mark sometimes appears to combine Matthew and Luke, mediating between them in wording. Yet in most cases Mark's vocabulary bears his own fingerprints and suggests originality rather than conflation: frequent *kai euthys* ("and immediately") and characteristically abrupt phrasing.

Major Contributors to the Theory

Although intimations of Mark's priority existed earlier, Karl Lachmann in 1835 was the first to argue systematically from Greek textual order that Mark's sequence was foundational. Christian Hermann Weisse and Heinrich Holtzmann elaborated the claim, pairing it with a second written source to form the Two-Source Hypothesis. In the early twentieth century, B. H. Streeter's *The Four Gospels* synthesized these arguments into a lasting model that combined Markan priority with additional sources M, L, and Q.

Later scholars tested and refined the theory with new methods. John C. Hawkins's *Horae Synopticae* quantified verbal parallels. Robert H. Stein, E. P. Sanders, and Margaret Davies articulated methodological criteria for detecting dependence. In the late twentieth century, Mark

Goodacre reaffirmed Markan priority within the Farrer framework (rejecting Q but retaining Mark first), while Frans Neirynck's exhaustive analysis of minor agreements pressed Two-Source advocates to nuance their conclusions. The enduring strength of the Markan-priority model lies in its capacity to incorporate such refinements without collapse. Whether combined with Q, as in the classic Two-Source view, or paired with the Farrer alternative that posits Luke's use of Matthew, Mark first remains the foundation stone.

Implications for the Study of the Gospels

Accepting Markan priority changes how readers approach all three Synoptic Gospels. It casts Mark as a creative theologian in his own right, not merely a condensed digest of Matthew or Luke. It allows Matthew and Luke to be studied as redactors who interpreted and extended Mark's narrative for their communities. It situates the Gospel tradition within a dynamic process of literary and theological development rather than static repetition.

Historically, this perspective supports the view that the earliest written portrayal of Jesus centered on proclamation of the kingdom and the mystery of his suffering and death. Theologically, it highlights the evangelists as interpreters inspired to adapt inherited material for new circumstances.

Conclusion

Markan priority is not a dogma but an explanatory framework. It remains persuasive because it accounts most simply for the observable facts: the sequence of events, the pattern of verbal agreement, the consistent editorial behavior of Matthew and Luke, and the trajectory of theological development. Every hypothesis faces anomalies, yet the cumulative weight of evidence continues to favor Mark as the earliest of the canonical Gospels.

Recognizing Mark's priority does not diminish the other evangelists; it illuminates their creativity. From Mark's terse proclamation, Matthew crafted an expanded catechetical Gospel for Jewish-Christian readers, and Luke composed a universal history stretching from Israel to the nations. The story that began with Mark's brief, urgent narrative would grow into a richly layered tradition, one that still invites study, faith, and wonder.

Chapter 5
The Q Hypothesis (Two-Source Theory)

The Place of Q in the Synoptic Discussion

The theory of Markan priority provides a compelling explanation for the structure and order of the Synoptic Gospels, but it does not by itself account for every literary relationship among them. When Mark's material is removed from Matthew and Luke, a significant body of shared material remains, totaling approximately two hundred to three hundred verses, that appears in both Matthew and Luke but is absent from Mark. This shared content includes some of the most memorable sayings of Jesus: the Beatitudes, the Lord's Prayer, the temptation narrative, the mission charge, and parables such as the Lost Sheep. The similarities in wording are often close, yet the sequence and setting of the material differ sharply.

This phenomenon, known as the double tradition, lies at the center of the Q hypothesis. The traditional explanation, often called the Two-Source Theory, holds that both Matthew and Luke independently used two written sources in composing their Gospels: Mark and another document, now lost, containing sayings and teachings of Jesus. This hypothetical second source is referred to simply as Q, from the German *Quelle*, meaning "source."

The Two-Source Theory became the dominant solution to the Synoptic Problem in the twentieth century because it explained two major phenomena at once: the extensive overlap among all three Synoptic Gospels (the triple tradition) and the large body of shared non-Markan material (the double tradition). The combination of Markan priority and Q offered an elegant and comprehensive framework for understanding both.

What Was Q?

The hypothetical document Q is usually described as a written collection of sayings and teachings of Jesus, perhaps arranged thematically rather than narratively. It likely included material such as the Sermon on the Mount or the Sermon on the Plain, the Beatitudes, the Lord's Prayer, the Temptation narrative, the parables of the Lost Sheep and the Great Feast, and numerous individual aphorisms and instructions. Q, as reconstructed by many scholars, lacks a Passion narrative and contains very few miracles.

If such a document existed, it represents one of the earliest attempts to preserve Jesus' words in written form. Unlike Mark's fast-moving narrative of deeds and conflicts, Q would reflect an early Christian community interested primarily in the teaching of Jesus and the wisdom of his message. It would portray Jesus as a prophetic teacher who calls for repentance, mercy, and faithfulness, a figure of both divine authority and moral challenge.

Many reconstructions divide Q into three sections: an introductory sequence involving John the Baptist and the Temptation of Jesus; a middle section of teaching material centered on discipleship, ethics, and divine wisdom; and a concluding collection of warnings and eschatological sayings. Although we have no physical manuscript of Q, the consistency of double-tradition parallels suggests that both Matthew and Luke drew on a shared written source with a recognizable structure.

Why Posit a Written Source?

The chief reason for proposing Q is the pattern of agreement between Matthew and Luke in the double tradition. The verbal similarity in many of these passages is too close to be explained by independent oral transmission. For instance, the wording of the Lord's Prayer and the sequence of beatitudes share so much overlap that coincidence is improbable.

If Luke had used Matthew directly, one might expect him to reproduce Matthew's order, but he does not. Matthew gathers sayings into five great discourses, especially the Sermon on the Mount, while Luke scatters similar material throughout his narrative, especially within the long "travel narrative" section (Lk 9–19). If Luke were copying Matthew, such radical rearrangement seems unlikely. However, if both evangelists independently drew from a sayings source, identified as Q, they could easily use the same material differently.

Furthermore, certain passages show alternating primitivity: at some points Matthew's version seems earlier, while at others Luke's appears more original. This oscillation suggests that neither author copied the other, but rather that each independently drew from a common source and adapted it freely. The hypothesis of a shared written source, therefore, provides a coherent explanation for both the similarities and differences between Matthew and Luke in the double tradition.

The Composition and Character of Q

The question of what Q looked like and how it was composed has generated substantial scholarship. B. H. Streeter envisioned Q as a written Greek document, roughly as long as the Gospel of Mark, consisting mainly of sayings of Jesus organized into groups or collections. He proposed that both Matthew and Luke had access to Q in written form and drew upon it independently.

Later research has refined this view. John S. Kloppenborg's influential analysis identified compositional layers within Q. He argued that the earliest stratum, which he calls Q^1, consists of wisdom and ethical sayings about poverty, nonviolence, and the proper use of wealth. These teachings portray Jesus as a sage or teacher of divine wisdom. A second layer, Q^2, adds prophetic and apocalyptic material, including warnings about judgment, the mission charge, and lamentations over unrepentant cities. A possible third layer, Q^3, provides brief narrative introductions or transitions that frame the sayings, such as the dialogue between John the Baptist and Jesus.

If Kloppenborg's reconstruction is correct, Q was not a static collection but a developing text, shaped over time by successive editors within an early Christian community. Its growth mirrors the community's reflection on Jesus' teaching and identity. This layered composition also explains the diversity of themes within the double tradition: some passages express wisdom ethics, others prophetic judgment, still others eschatological expectation.

The Q Community

The existence of Q implies an early Christian community centered on the preservation and interpretation of Jesus' teachings. Scholars such as James M. Robinson and Burton L. Mack developed this sociological perspective, suggesting that Q reflects a group of Jesus-followers who treasured his words but did not yet emphasize his death and resurrection. For them, Jesus was primarily the inspired teacher and prophet of divine wisdom, whose message called for moral transformation and radical trust in God.

In this reading, the Q community represents a distinctive stream within early Christianity, one that emphasized sayings rather than narrative, teaching rather than passion, and discipleship rather than dogma. Although this model is speculative, it has helped scholars imagine the diverse theological landscapes that characterized the first generations of Christian believers. The Q tradition, if it existed, preserved one such voice within the chorus of early Christian proclamation.

Challenges to the Q Hypothesis

Despite its enduring influence, the Q hypothesis faces several serious challenges. The first and most obvious is that no manuscript evidence for Q exists. No ancient writer quotes or mentions a sayings collection corresponding to it, and no fragment resembling it has been found among early Christian papyri. Critics argue that this absence of physical or historical evidence makes Q an unnecessary and overly hypothetical construct.

Advocates respond that the absence of manuscripts is not decisive. Many early Christian writings have been lost, and the disappearance of a document is not surprising in a period of fragile textual transmission. Q may have been absorbed into Matthew and Luke and thus rendered obsolete. The same is true of other early texts known only indirectly, such as the Signs Gospel hypothesized within John or early versions of the *Didache*.

A second challenge concerns the minor agreements between Matthew and Luke against Mark within triple-tradition passages. These agreements, which are small shared omissions or additions, seem to suggest that Matthew and Luke knew each other's texts. Proponents of Q, however, note that most of these minor agreements can be explained by common editorial tendencies or later scribal harmonization. The evidence is intriguing but not decisive against Q.

A third objection points to the difficulty of imagining Luke's radical rearrangement of Matthew if he had Matthew before him. Proponents of the Farrer Hypothesis argue that Luke could have reorganized Matthew's material to suit his own literary design. Yet supporters of Q reply that Luke's distinctive order makes more sense if he worked from an independent source rather than dismantling an existing Gospel.

The Two-Source Theory in Modern Scholarship

The Two-Source Theory reached its mature form in the work of B. H. Streeter in *The Four Gospels* (1924). Streeter's synthesis proposed four sources as the foundation of the Synoptic tradition: Mark, Q, M (special Matthew), and L (special Luke). This framework dominated critical study for much of the twentieth century.

Subsequent scholarship refined but did not displace the model. The International Q Project, begun in the late twentieth century, undertook a systematic reconstruction of Q, producing a *Critical Edition of Q* with textual apparatus and commentary. Kloppenborg, Tuckett, and others analyzed Q's theology and social context, while scholars such as Robinson and Mack interpreted Q as a window into early Christian movements that emphasized Jesus as a teacher of wisdom.

Even those who question Q's existence acknowledge that the Two-Source Theory remains methodologically fruitful. It provides a consistent framework for exploring the relationships among the Synoptics, and it continues to stimulate debate and testing of alternative models such as the Farrer and Griesbach hypotheses.

Theological and Historical Implications

If Q existed, it represents a remarkable stage in the development of early Christian thought. It would be one of the earliest attempts to organize Jesus' teachings into a coherent written form. Its emphasis on ethical instruction and divine wisdom complements the apocalyptic urgency of Mark and the narrative and theological expansions of Matthew and Luke.

Theologically, Q underscores the diversity of early Christian witness. It suggests that before the passion narrative became central, Jesus was remembered primarily as a teacher who proclaimed God's kingdom in words. Historically, Q shows that the early church was not monolithic but included communities that preserved different aspects of Jesus' identity and mission.

Even if Q never existed as a distinct document, the double tradition still preserves this early layer of teaching. Whether drawn from a written source or from oral collections, these sayings continue to give voice to the earliest memories of Jesus' words and wisdom.

Evaluation

The Q hypothesis remains both influential and contested. Its strength lies in its explanatory power. It accounts for the close verbal similarity of

Matthew and Luke in the double tradition, their differing arrangement of material, and their alternating primitivity. It offers a coherent framework that preserves the independence of both evangelists while explaining their overlap.

Its weakness lies in its hypothetical nature. Q is a reconstruction, not an artifact. The theory is open to modification, and alternative models such as the Farrer Hypothesis challenge the necessity of positing a lost source. Yet even if future scholarship were to move beyond Q, the questions it raises about the preservation of Jesus' teachings, the diversity of early Christian communities, and the literary creativity of the evangelists would remain.

Conclusion

The Q hypothesis stands as one of the most enduring and provocative ideas in modern New Testament study. Whether one accepts it or not, it has profoundly shaped how scholars understand the formation of the Gospels and the transmission of Jesus' words. The Two-Source Theory, combining Markan priority and Q, continues to serve as the dominant framework for explaining the relationships among Matthew, Mark, and Luke. For interpreters and students, Q invites both caution and imagination. It reminds readers that the written Gospels stand upon earlier traditions (spoken, remembered, and perhaps written) that circulated in the first decades of the Christian movement. The search for Q is ultimately a search for the earliest voices that bore witness to Jesus. In that sense, the quest for Q, even if the document itself remains elusive, continues to illuminate the complex and living process by which the Gospel tradition came into being.

Chapter 6
The Farrer Hypothesis (No-Q)

The Emergence of an Alternative

For nearly a century, the Two-Source Theory held unrivaled sway as the dominant solution to the Synoptic Problem. By combining Markan priority with the postulation of a sayings source called Q, it offered an elegant and apparently complete explanation for both the triple and double traditions. Yet not all scholars have been convinced of the necessity of an invisible document, one for which no manuscript, citation, or clear historical trace exists. Out of this concern grew a series of arguments that eventually converged in what is now known as the Farrer Hypothesis.

Named for Austin Farrer, whose 1955 essay *On Dispensing with Q* first articulated its modern form, this hypothesis affirms Markan priority but rejects the need for Q. It holds instead that Luke knew and used both Mark and Matthew directly. The Farrer Hypothesis thus preserves one of the key insights of modern criticism, that Mark was first, while simplifying the traditional Two-Source model by removing an unnecessary layer of speculation.

Farrer's proposal built on a basic methodological principle: do not multiply entities beyond necessity. If the observable data can be explained through known documents, there is no reason to invent an unknown one. This appeal to parsimony has made the hypothesis attractive to those who prefer arguments grounded in textual evidence rather than in hypothetical reconstruction.

The Basic Outline of the Hypothesis

The Farrer Hypothesis stands on three main claims. First, Mark was the earliest Gospel, written around the late 60s CE, providing the narrative foundation for both Matthew and Luke. Second, Matthew used Mark as his primary source, supplementing it with additional material, some written, some oral, and shaping the result into a catechetical work organized around five major teaching discourses. Third, Luke, writing somewhat later, also used Mark but knew Matthew's Gospel as well. He incorporated and rearranged Matthew's sayings material within his own narrative framework, often modifying it to suit his distinctive theological vision.

In this model, the double tradition (i.e., material shared by Matthew and Luke but absent from Mark) is not derived from a lost sayings source. Instead, it represents Luke's direct borrowing from Matthew, whether by excerpting entire sections or by distributing individual sayings throughout his Gospel.

This simple sequence (Mark → Matthew → Luke) requires no hypothetical Q, no reconstructed textual layers, and no lost community documents. It depends only on the three canonical Gospels themselves and the assumption that Luke, as a careful historian (cf. Lk 1:1–4), was aware of earlier written accounts, including Matthew.

Evidence for Luke's Use of Matthew

Several kinds of evidence lend support to the idea that Luke knew Matthew's Gospel. One of the most prominent is the phenomenon of minor agreements: small instances where Matthew and Luke agree in wording or detail against Mark within triple-tradition material. Examples include shared omissions, added words, or harmonizing phrases. These agreements are difficult to explain if Matthew and Luke were entirely independent, as the Two-Source Theory asserts, but they make perfect sense if Luke had access to Matthew's text.

Another piece of evidence is the presence of doublets in Luke: parallel sayings or episodes that appear twice in slightly different forms. For example, the saying about the lamp under a bushel occurs in both Luke 8:16 and 11:33, while the parable of the Talents reappears as the parable of the Pounds (Lk 19:12–27). Michael Goulder argued that such doublets arise naturally if Luke had two written sources (i.e., Mark and Matthew) and chose to preserve both versions of similar material rather than harmonizing them.

Finally, Luke's editorial patterns often reflect dependence on Matthew. In several places, Luke begins with Mark's version of a story but inserts or modifies elements that appear in Matthew. The temptation narrative provides an instructive example. Matthew and Luke share the same three temptations in slightly different order.

If Luke used Matthew, his reordering of the second and third temptations makes perfect sense as a literary choice emphasizing the temple in Jerusalem as the geographical and theological climax of his Gospel.

The Argument from Parsimony

At the heart of Farrer's proposal is the principle of parsimony, often summarized as "Occam's razor." If the same data can be explained by fewer assumptions, the simpler explanation is to be preferred. The Two-Source Theory requires not only Mark and Matthew but also a hypothetical document, Q, for which there is no direct evidence. The Farrer Hypothesis, by contrast, explains the same phenomena using only the three Gospels we already possess.

Austin Farrer argued that the intellectual appeal of Q rested not on evidence but on convenience. Q allowed scholars to preserve the independence of Matthew and Luke and to postulate an early sayings tradition without confronting the literary relationship between the two Gospels. Yet the independence of Matthew and Luke, he suggested, is itself an assumption rather than a fact. If Luke's prologue acknowledges that "many have undertaken to set down an account," it is entirely plausible that one of those earlier accounts was Matthew.

This argument persuaded later scholars, including Goulder and Mark Goodacre, who developed Farrer's insights with detailed literary analysis. They contended that Luke's distinctive patterns of dependence, editing, and rearrangement correspond closely to what one would expect from a writer adapting both Mark and Matthew.

The Role of Editorial Fatigue

A particularly striking line of argument comes from the study of editorial fatigue, a concept popularized by Mark Goodacre. Editorial fatigue occurs when an author begins to adapt a source but forgets the changes made, inadvertently reverting to the wording or logic of the original. Such moments betray direct literary dependence because they reveal the process of editing in motion.

One example occurs in the parable of the Talents (Mt 25:14–30) and its Lukan counterpart, the parable of the Pounds (Lk 19:11–27). Luke begins by modifying Matthew's setting, turning the parable into a story about a nobleman who goes to receive a kingdom. Yet as the narrative unfolds, Luke retains details that fit Matthew's original version better than his own new context. The effect is that of a writer who has altered a story but unconsciously slipped back into his source.

Another instance appears in the story of the rejection at Nazareth (Mk 6:1–6; Mt 13:53–58; Lk 4:16–30). Luke moves the episode to the beginning of Jesus' ministry, transforming it into a programmatic sermon in the synagogue. Yet as the story progresses, details remain that presuppose its later position in Mark and Matthew. Luke's placement of the account before the calling of the disciples produces small inconsistencies, which is an example of editorial fatigue revealing dependence on earlier material.

Such phenomena are difficult to explain on the Two-Source model but align naturally with Luke's direct use of Matthew.

Order and the Travel Narrative

The most persistent objection to the Farrer Hypothesis concerns Luke's arrangement of material. If Luke had Matthew before him, why did he not simply adopt Matthew's order? Instead of preserving Matthew's five discourses, Luke redistributes the sayings throughout his long travel narrative (Lk 9:51–19:27).

Farrer advocates respond that Luke's reorganization is entirely consistent with his literary and theological aims. Luke's Gospel is a journey from Galilee to Jerusalem, symbolizing Jesus' mission to bring salvation from Israel to the nations. By embedding Matthew's sayings into this travel framework, Luke integrates teaching and journey into a single theological motif. The rearrangement therefore testifies not to independence but to creative adaptation.

Michael Goulder emphasized that Luke was not merely a compiler but a deliberate author who shaped inherited material according to a unifying design. His decision to scatter Matthew's sayings was purposeful, not random, reflecting his intention to present Jesus as the traveling prophet whose ministry unfolds under divine direction toward the culmination of the cross and resurrection.

Strengths of the Farrer Hypothesis

The Farrer Hypothesis offers several strengths that commend it to consideration. It eliminates the need for a hypothetical document, relying only on extant evidence. It explains the minor agreements, doublets, and editorial patterns with economy. It portrays Luke as a highly literate theologian engaging both Mark and Matthew in creative dialogue. And it aligns well with Luke's own preface, which acknowledges multiple earlier accounts as sources for his work.

Moreover, the Farrer model restores a sense of literary continuity among the Gospels. Rather than envisioning three independent authors drawing separately from a now-lost source, it imagines a living chain of composition in which each evangelist reads, edits, and reinterprets his predecessors. This approach emphasizes the human artistry of the Gospel writers and the theological richness of their interrelationship.

Finally, by removing Q, the Farrer Hypothesis invites renewed attention to Matthew and Luke as interpreters of one another. The study of how Luke read and transformed Matthew's Gospel can illuminate both texts, revealing the creativity of early Christian storytelling.

Weaknesses and Continuing Debates

Despite its elegance, the Farrer Hypothesis faces significant challenges. Many scholars remain unconvinced that Luke would have used Matthew as freely as the theory requires. Luke's rearrangement of sayings material is so extensive that some find it more plausible to assume independent use of a common source rather than direct dependence. Furthermore, certain features of the double tradition seem difficult to explain by Luke's use of Matthew alone, such as alternating primitivity, where sometimes Matthew's version appears earlier and sometimes Luke's.

Critics also question whether Luke's theology would have permitted such extensive modification of Matthew. Luke's careful preface and stylistic polish suggest respect for sources, yet the Farrer model implies that he disassembled one of them almost beyond recognition. Advocates respond that such freedom was not unusual in the ancient world, where rewriting and recontextualizing sources was a common literary practice.

Finally, the Farrer Hypothesis does not easily account for all of the material unique to Matthew and Luke (the so-called M and L material). While these may derive from oral tradition or from additional written sources, their existence reminds scholars that the composition of the Gospels was more complex than any single linear model can fully describe.

Major Contributors and Scholarly Development

Austin Farrer's brief essay provided the conceptual foundation for the hypothesis, but it was Michael Goulder who transformed it into a comprehensive model through his studies of Luke's redactional method, especially in *Midrash and Lection in Matthew* (1974) and *Luke: A New*

Paradigm (1989). Goulder's meticulous analysis of Lukan doublets, structure, and theology sought to demonstrate that Luke's Gospel was not dependent on hypothetical sources but on the tangible texts of Mark and Matthew.

In recent decades, Mark Goodacre has become the leading advocate of the Farrer Hypothesis. His *The Case Against Q* (2002) and *The Synoptic Problem: A Way Through the Maze* (2001) offer clear, concise arguments showing that the existence of Q is unnecessary once Luke's use of Matthew is acknowledged. Goodacre's emphasis on editorial fatigue, stylistic coherence, and parsimony has revitalized discussion and ensured that the Farrer model remains a central contender in Synoptic studies.

Other scholars, while not embracing Farrer's conclusions wholesale, have found his approach methodologically attractive. By focusing on observable textual phenomena rather than speculative reconstructions, the Farrer school has encouraged renewed attention to literary analysis, authorial intention, and the artistry of composition within the Gospels themselves.

Theological and Hermeneutical Implications

The Farrer Hypothesis has implications that extend beyond literary theory. It reshapes how readers understand Luke's theological creativity and the process of Gospel formation. If Luke knew both Mark and Matthew, then his Gospel stands as the culmination of a deliberate and thoughtful engagement with prior tradition. Luke becomes not only a historian but also a theologian who rereads the story of Jesus in light of earlier written testimonies.

This perspective also affects how the Church interprets the Gospels collectively. The canonical arrangement (i.e., Matthew, Mark, Luke) may not represent chronological sequence, but it symbolizes the cumulative development of the tradition. The Farrer model highlights that development as an ongoing theological conversation rather than a series of isolated compositions.

For theology, this means that inspiration operates through continuity and reinterpretation as much as through originality. The Gospel writers were not passive recorders but active interpreters who shaped their sources in faith. Luke's Gospel, read through this lens, emerges as a rich synthesis of narrative, teaching, and theology. And the Third Gospel stands out as a Gospel of maturity reflecting both dependence and innovation.

Evaluation

The Farrer Hypothesis deserves respect for its clarity and restraint. It eliminates the speculative element of a lost document while preserving the established results of Markan priority. It treats Luke as an intelligent, creative author rather than as a compiler of fragments. Its appeal lies in its simplicity and in its fidelity to known evidence.

Yet it is not without its difficulties. Explaining Luke's dramatic rearrangement of Matthew's material remains challenging, and some double-tradition passages fit awkwardly within the framework. The Farrer model may simplify the documentary scheme but does not dissolve all complexity. Still, as an alternative to the Two-Source Theory, it compels ongoing reexamination of inherited assumptions and encourages scholars to test every claim against the text itself.

Conclusion

The Farrer Hypothesis represents a significant and enduring voice in modern discussion of the Synoptic Problem. It demonstrates that critical study of the Gospels can proceed without reliance on hypothetical sources and that close literary analysis can yield profound insight into the evangelists' artistry.

Whether or not it ultimately prevails, the hypothesis has reshaped the conversation. It reminds interpreters that the Gospels are not static records but dynamic works of theology and imagination, written in creative response to one another. If Luke indeed read Matthew, then the third evangelist stands as both heir and innovator: one who received tradition, reinterpreted it, and in doing so, carried the story of Jesus forward into new contexts and new generations.

Chapter 7
The Griesbach / Two-Gospel Hypothesis

The Historical Setting of the Proposal

Among the several solutions proposed to the Synoptic Problem, one of the oldest and most resilient is known as the Griesbach Hypothesis, or more recently, the Two-Gospel Hypothesis. This model reverses the assumptions of the Two-Source Theory and offers an alternative sequence of dependence: Matthew wrote first, Luke used Matthew, and Mark wrote last, condensing and combining the two.

The origins of this theory lie in the late eighteenth century. Johann Jakob Griesbach, a German scholar of the Enlightenment, published his *Synopsis* of the Gospels in 1776, providing for the first time a detailed parallel-column comparison of the Synoptic texts. This innovation allowed scholars to observe the precise relationships between the Gospels. On the basis of his analysis, Griesbach argued that Matthew was written first, Luke wrote with Matthew before him, and Mark drew from both. His argument stood in deliberate contrast to the growing trend toward Markan priority that would dominate later scholarship.

Griesbach's proposal was not merely a defense of tradition. It reflected a careful reading of the data available to him. Because Matthew occupied the first position in the canonical order and was often regarded by the early Church as the earliest Gospel, Griesbach found it natural to begin there. He noted that Luke frequently agreed with Matthew in order and content, though with differences of style and emphasis. Mark, in his view, appeared to abbreviate or conflate these two earlier accounts.

The Core Structure of the Hypothesis

The Two-Gospel Hypothesis begins with the traditional assumption that the apostle Matthew composed his Gospel first, perhaps in the context of the early Jewish-Christian mission. Matthew's Gospel, rich in Old Testament quotations and organized teaching material, served as a comprehensive handbook for the early Church. Luke, writing somewhat later, composed his Gospel with knowledge of Matthew, supplementing it with other traditions available to him, some oral and perhaps some written. Luke's aim, as stated in his prologue, was to produce an orderly account that would reassure his readers of the truth of the traditions they had received.

Mark, writing after both Matthew and Luke, drew from these two predecessors to create a concise and powerful narrative. He selected, abridged, and reworded material from each, often preserving the vivid language of Luke while following the general outline of Matthew. The result was a Gospel of action and immediacy, shorter but more dramatic than its sources.

This model, therefore, envisions a literary sequence that moves from Matthew to Luke to Mark, with each successive evangelist shaping inherited material for new audiences and purposes.

The Revival of the Griesbach Hypothesis

For much of the nineteenth and early twentieth centuries, Griesbach's theory remained a historical curiosity overshadowed by the Two-Source model. The revival came in the mid-twentieth century, largely through the work of William R. Farmer. Farmer's 1964 book *The Synoptic Problem: A Critical Analysis* argued that the case for Markan priority was far less secure than its widespread acceptance suggested. He contended that the evidence could be equally, and sometimes better, explained by the Griesbach sequence.

Farmer emphasized that the Two-Gospel Hypothesis restored continuity with the testimony of early Christian tradition, especially that of Augustine, who had proposed a similar order in *De Consensu Evangelistarum.* Augustine wrote that Matthew was first, Mark followed as Matthew's "abbreviator," and Luke composed his Gospel with knowledge of both. The Griesbach model, Farmer argued, harmonized the best elements of historical tradition with a plausible literary explanation.

In the decades that followed, a number of scholars joined Farmer in developing and defending this approach, including Bernard Orchard, Harold Riley, and David Dungan. Collectively, they presented a coherent challenge to the dominance of Markan priority and invited a new generation of interpreters to reconsider long-held assumptions.

Arguments in Favor of the Two-Gospel Hypothesis

Supporters of the Griesbach model marshal several lines of argument. One is the theological and literary primacy of Matthew. Matthew's Gospel contains a fully developed ecclesiology, a systematic teaching structure, and a balanced narrative that moves from infancy to resurrection. Its use of Old Testament fulfillment citations and its emphasis on Jesus as the teacher of righteousness suggest that it was designed to serve as a foundational document for the early Church. This internal evidence, combined with ancient testimony that Matthew wrote first, lends historical plausibility to the model.

A second argument concerns the relationship between Matthew and Luke. The Two-Gospel Hypothesis posits direct literary dependence between these two Gospels without recourse to Q. Advocates point out that Luke's preface explicitly acknowledges the existence of earlier written accounts. If Matthew's Gospel was already circulating, Luke's use of it is not only possible but probable. Luke appears to borrow from Matthew's structure but to revise it for his own theological ends, such as emphasizing the inclusion of Gentiles and the universal scope of salvation.

A third line of reasoning centers on Mark's character in terms of conflation. Mark's Gospel is shorter than both Matthew and Luke, yet it often contains the most vivid details. Proponents of the Two-Gospel Hypothesis interpret this not as evidence of originality but as the mark of a skillful abridger who selected striking material from his sources. Where Matthew and Luke diverge, Mark often presents a version that seems to blend elements of both. This pattern, they argue, fits more naturally if Mark used the two as sources rather than serving as their source.

The Question of Order and Dependence

A central feature of the Griesbach model is the claim that Mark's sequence of events is derived from Matthew and Luke rather than vice versa. When Matthew and Luke agree in order, Mark follows them; when they differ, Mark tends to choose one or to weave the two together. For instance, in the order of episodes surrounding the feeding of the five thousand and the walking on the sea, Mark appears to adopt Matthew's sequence while incorporating Lukan detail.

Supporters of the hypothesis contend that this pattern shows Mark's dependence. They also note that Mark's omissions (such as the infancy narratives, many parables, and large portions of teaching material) can be explained by the evangelist's intent to produce a concise narrative focused on Jesus' deeds. Such a purpose would naturally lead him to omit long discourses and to concentrate on action.

Critics of Markan priority often ask why, if Mark wrote first, two later evangelists would have expanded his Gospel so differently yet both preserved his structure so faithfully. The Two-Gospel model, by contrast, envisions Mark summarizing the two longer works already in circulation, which would naturally result in the combination of their shared material and the omission of what was unique to each.

Challenges and Criticisms

The Two-Gospel Hypothesis, though revived with vigor, has faced sustained critique from defenders of Markan priority. The most significant objection is that the theory requires a highly selective Mark who managed to condense and combine Matthew and Luke while preserving remarkable verbal agreement with both. The precision of Mark's wording in many places suggests that he could hardly have maintained such balance without either copying one Gospel directly or having a level of literary craftsmanship unparalleled in ancient composition.

Another challenge concerns the minor agreements of Matthew and Luke against Mark. While Two-Gospel advocates interpret these as evidence of Luke's use of Matthew, critics point out that such agreements are often small and unevenly distributed. The Two-Source Theory explains them as textual or editorial phenomena rather than as signs of direct literary dependence.

A further difficulty lies in the historical chronology implied by the Two-Gospel Hypothesis. It requires Mark to have written last, yet some early patristic testimony, as well as internal evidence, suggests that Mark's Gospel was known relatively early, perhaps in the 60s CE. Reconciling this with Matthew and Luke's composition dates demands careful adjustment of historical timelines.

Theological and Hermeneutical Considerations

Beyond the question of order and dependence lies a deeper issue: what does the Two-Gospel Hypothesis suggest about the nature of the Gospels themselves? If Matthew was first, his Gospel stands as the primary theological expression of early Christianity, presenting Jesus as the fulfillment of Israel's story and the teacher of the new covenant. Luke's use of Matthew would then represent a broadening of this theological vision, extending salvation to Gentiles and situating the Gospel within a universal history of God's work.

Mark's contribution, in this view, is the condensation of both earlier works into a single dramatic narrative focused on action, urgency, and the suffering Messiah. Theologically, Mark would not be the primitive source behind Matthew and Luke but a theologian who interpreted and reshaped their portraits of Jesus for his own audience.

This model, therefore, portrays the Gospel tradition as a progression from the comprehensive teaching of Matthew, through Luke's inclusive retelling, to Mark's compact proclamation of the Gospel's core. It underscores continuity rather than divergence among the Synoptics, suggesting that they developed organically within a living tradition rather than as competing literary projects.

Major Contributors and Continuing Discussion

Following William Farmer's work, several scholars expanded the argument and applied it to specific Synoptic passages. Bernard Orchard developed the proposal within a Catholic context, emphasizing its harmony with early Church testimony and with the theological unity of the Gospels. Harold Riley explored its implications for understanding the formation of the canon. David Dungan contributed major studies on the history of Gospel criticism, showing how philosophical presuppositions of nineteenth-century scholarship favored Markan priority over alternative models.

These scholars, often working collaboratively, demonstrated that the Two-Gospel Hypothesis could be defended with historical rigor and textual sensitivity. Their collective efforts produced new synopses and analytical tools designed to test the hypothesis against the evidence. Although the Two-Gospel model remains a minority position, it continues to attract thoughtful advocates who value its alignment with early tradition and its capacity to explain certain textual phenomena more intuitively than the Two-Source Theory.

Evaluation of the Two-Gospel Hypothesis

The Two-Gospel Hypothesis stands as both a challenge and a corrective to the assumptions of modern source criticism. Its primary strength lies in its respect for ancient tradition and its refusal to multiply hypothetical documents. It highlights the possibility that the early Church's memory of Gospel order (i.e., Matthew, Luke, Mark) may not have been mistaken. It also offers an attractive vision of literary and theological development within the canonical sequence.

Yet the theory faces formidable difficulties. The linguistic and stylistic evidence continues to support Markan priority for many scholars. The precision of verbal agreement between Mark and the other Synoptics, the roughness of Mark's style, and the direction of redactional changes are often more easily explained if Mark wrote first. Moreover, the Two-Gospel model struggles to account for the extensive Markan material that both Matthew and Luke share while diverging elsewhere.

Nevertheless, the Griesbach or Two-Gospel Hypothesis endures because it keeps open the essential question of method. It reminds scholars that the evidence of the Synoptic Gospels can support more than one coherent reconstruction and that assumptions inherited from previous generations must continually be tested.

Conclusion

The revival of the Griesbach Hypothesis through Farmer and his successors has ensured that discussion of the Synoptic Problem remains a living field of inquiry rather than a closed case. By insisting that Matthew and Luke came before Mark, the Two-Gospel Hypothesis reverses the direction of dependence assumed by most modern scholarship and calls interpreters to reexamine both textual evidence and theological implications.

Even if one ultimately favors Markan priority, engagement with the Two-Gospel model sharpens understanding of the data and exposes the interpretive choices underlying every hypothesis. Like all serious contributions to Synoptic study, it presses scholars to hold historical, literary, and theological considerations together in a single vision. In this way, the Griesbach or Two-Gospel Hypothesis continues to serve as a vital conversation partner, ensuring that the Synoptic Problem remains what it has always been: a question that invites fresh reflection on the nature of the Gospels and on the remarkable story they tell.

Chapter 8
The Augustinian Hypothesis and Other Models

Historical Background and Context

The Augustinian Hypothesis holds a special place in the history of Synoptic study. It represents the earliest articulated theory of Gospel relationships and, for more than a millennium, was accepted almost without question in both the Western and Eastern Churches. Long before the rise of modern critical methods, early Christian writers sought to explain the similarities and differences among the four canonical Gospels in ways consistent with faith and tradition. Their reflections were guided less by textual comparison and more by theological coherence and the conviction that the evangelists wrote under divine inspiration.

In this traditional understanding, Matthew was written first, Mark second, and Luke third, with each later evangelist drawing upon the earlier ones. The fourth Gospel, John, was understood to stand apart as a more spiritual and theological work. This order of composition, affirmed by Augustine in the early fifth century, became the standard account for over a thousand years and shaped how generations of readers understood the relationships among the Synoptic Gospels.

Augustine's Theory in *De Consensu Evangelistarum*

In his treatise *De Consensu Evangelistarum* ("On the Harmony of the Evangelists"), written around 400 CE, Augustine of Hippo offered the first systematic discussion of Gospel origins. Augustine sought to show that the four Gospels do not contradict one another but rather form a coherent, divinely inspired witness to Christ. To explain their differences, he proposed a sequence of dependence that preserved both harmony and individuality.

According to Augustine, Matthew wrote first, guided by his experience as an apostle and directed primarily toward a Jewish audience. Mark, described as a follower and "interpreter" of Peter, used Matthew as his primary source but abbreviated it for a Roman readership. Luke, writing later, drew upon both Matthew and Mark, composing a more orderly account addressed to Gentile believers. John, finally, wrote last, offering a theological reflection that supplemented and deepened the Synoptic narratives.

Augustine's view is strikingly close to what would later be called the Griesbach or Two-Gospel Hypothesis, though it preceded modern literary analysis by more than a millennium. His concern was not source criticism as such but theological coherence. He assumed that the evangelists wrote in succession, each aware of his predecessors, guided by the Holy Spirit to emphasize different dimensions of the same truth.

Reception and Enduring Influence

For centuries, the Augustinian sequence of the New Testament Gospels (i.e., Matthew, Mark, Luke, John) was treated as a fact of sacred history. The early Church Fathers, medieval theologians, and Renaissance scholars alike assumed that Matthew's Gospel stood first, in part because of its position at the head of the New Testament canon and in part because of its strong connection to apostolic authority. Mark's dependence on Matthew was considered self-evident, and Luke's preface was read as confirming his awareness of prior written accounts.

Even after the rise of historical criticism, the Augustinian order retained an enduring influence. Many church traditions, particularly within Roman Catholic and Orthodox contexts, continued to view it as both plausible and theologically satisfying. In the nineteenth century, when German scholars began to favor Markan priority, others defended the older view as a safeguard of apostolic continuity. Its persistence across centuries demonstrates how deeply the question of Gospel order intertwines with matters of faith, authority, and canon.

The Augustinian Hypothesis Reconsidered in Modern Scholarship

The modern revival of interest in the Augustinian model parallels the rediscovery of the Griesbach Hypothesis, with which it shares important features. Like Griesbach, it posits Matthew's priority and Mark's dependence on

Matthew. However, it differs in one crucial respect: whereas Griesbach argued that Luke used Matthew and Mark used both, Augustine proposed that Luke used Matthew and Mark, but Mark also drew from Matthew directly. The result is a more complex web of interdependence, in which each Synoptic writer engages both predecessors.

Twentieth-century scholars such as John Wenham and David Alan Black revisited the Augustinian Hypothesis, arguing that its early attestation and theological coherence deserve renewed consideration. Wenham's *Redating Matthew, Mark, and Luke* (1992) combined historical reasoning with textual analysis to suggest that the traditional order could fit the available evidence as well as, or better than, models based on Markan priority. These scholars did not claim that Augustine's proposal should simply replace modern theories, but that it should be taken seriously as an enduring alternative.

The Augustinian Hypothesis also appeals to those who view the early Church's memory as a form of historical evidence in its own right. If the earliest generations of Christians consistently believed that Matthew was written first and that Mark drew from him, this testimony deserves careful consideration alongside textual data. Modern historical methods, they argue, should not dismiss early tradition too quickly.

Evaluating the Augustinian Sequence

The primary strength of the Augustinian Hypothesis lies in its historical continuity. It represents the Church's earliest explicit reflection on the order of the Gospels and remained virtually uncontested for more than a thousand years. It provides a simple, intuitive explanation of dependence that respects the canonical sequence and honors the early testimonies of Papias, Irenaeus, and other Church Fathers.

Another strength is its theological coherence. The Augustinian order mirrors the canonical arrangement, suggesting a progression from the fulfillment-oriented Gospel of Matthew to the universal outreach of Luke. It situates Mark as a concise interpreter who captures the essentials of apostolic preaching for a wider audience. For many readers, this sequence maintains the unity of Scripture and the complementarity of the fourfold Gospel witness.

Yet, the Augustinian Hypothesis faces significant challenges from modern critical analysis. Its reliance on tradition rather than textual evidence makes it difficult to test by modern criteria. The phenomenon of Mark's rough style, vivid detail, and apparent primitivity remains more easily explained if Mark wrote first. Furthermore, the extensive verbal agreement between Mark and both Matthew and Luke suggests that Mark was not an independent abridgment but rather the common source on which the others depended. While Augustine's sequence provides a coherent theological framework, it struggles to account for the precise literary data revealed by side-by-side comparison of the Greek texts.

Alternative and Hybrid Proposals

Modern scholarship has generated numerous variations and hybrid models that seek to reconcile elements of the Augustinian tradition with the insights of critical analysis. One such approach is the Neo-Augustinian Hypothesis, which maintains Matthew's priority but suggests that Mark and Luke drew independently from Matthew rather than from each other. This model preserves the traditional starting point while acknowledging that the evangelists could have used common oral and written traditions alongside the first Gospel.

Another alternative is the Modified Two-Gospel Hypothesis, which blends features of both the Augustinian and Griesbach models. In this proposal, Matthew is first, Luke uses Matthew, and Mark draws on both but with additional influence from oral tradition and early catechetical summaries. Such hybrid models reflect an increasing willingness among scholars to recognize the complexity of the data and the possibility that no single linear sequence can account for every feature of the Synoptic relationship.

Digital tools and computational analyses have recently added new dimensions to the discussion. Stylometric studies, for example, have been used to test the direction of dependence between the Gospels based on statistical patterns of vocabulary and syntax. While results remain inconclusive, they illustrate how traditional hypotheses like Augustine's can continue to inspire fresh inquiry in light of modern methods.

Broader Theological and Hermeneutical Implications

The Augustinian Hypothesis, and the traditional order it represents, invites reflection on how theological convictions shape the study of Scripture. For Augustine and for many who followed him, the question of Gospel order was not merely literary but spiritual. It concerned the divine orchestration of revelation and the harmony of apostolic witness. Each evangelist, in this view, built upon his predecessors not as a mere compiler but as a fellow laborer inspired by the same Spirit.

Modern readers may approach the question differently, yet the theological insight remains relevant. The notion that the evangelists stand in continuity rather than competition affirms the integrity of the canonical Gospel collection. Whether or not one accepts Augustine's sequence, the hypothesis underscores the unity of purpose that binds Matthew, Mark, and Luke together: the proclamation of the one Gospel through multiple voices.

Evaluation

The Augustinian Hypothesis occupies a unique position among the competing explanations of the Synoptic Problem. It is both ancient and enduring, conservative and yet open to modern reappraisal. Its enduring appeal lies in its simplicity, its alignment with early tradition, and its affirmation of the canonical order as meaningful rather than arbitrary. It reminds scholars that the study of the Synoptics involves not only literary analysis but also historical memory and theological interpretation.

At the same time, the Augustinian model cannot escape the challenges posed by the textual evidence that gave rise to modern criticism. The patterns of verbal agreement, the stylistic primitivity of Mark, and the logic of redactional development remain persuasive reasons for favoring Markan priority. The Augustinian sequence, while historically venerable, struggles to account for these features without invoking complex and sometimes circular reasoning.

Nevertheless, the continuing interest in Augustine's theory demonstrates the value of plural perspectives. Each hypothesis (Two-Source, Farrer, Griesbach, or Augustinian) illuminates certain aspects of the Synoptic relationship while leaving others unresolved. The diversity of explanations is itself a sign of the richness of the Gospel tradition and the depth of the mystery it seeks to describe.

Conclusion

The Augustinian Hypothesis serves as a reminder that the investigation of the Synoptic Problem is both historical and theological. Augustine's vision of successive evangelists building upon one another to produce a harmonious fourfold Gospel may not satisfy every modern criterion of literary dependence, but it continues to capture the imagination of readers who see in the canon a providential unity.

In the end, the enduring significance of the Augustinian model lies less in its precise sequence than in the theological intuition it embodies: that the evangelists, guided by the same Spirit, bear witness together to the one Gospel of Jesus Christ. As scholarship continues to refine its methods and test its theories, Augustine's ancient insight continues to echo. It is a call to read the Synoptics not only as sources to be dissected but as voices in concert, proclaiming the same good news in diverse and complementary ways.

Part III
Evidence and Testing

Chapter 9
Evidence in Practice

Scope and Position in the Argument

The preceding chapters have explored the major hypotheses that attempt to explain the literary relationships among the Synoptic Gospels: Markan Priority, the Two-Source Theory with Q, the Farrer Hypothesis, the Griesbach or Two-Gospel Hypothesis, and the Augustinian Hypothesis. Each model has its own logic, particular strengths, and persistent weaknesses. Yet abstract theories cannot stand alone; they must be tested against the evidence of the texts themselves.

The real test of any solution to the Synoptic Problem is its ability to explain the similarities and differences in wording, order, and theology when specific passages are examined side by side. This chapter turns from theory to practice, presenting five worked examples that illustrate how each hypothesis interprets the same material. By applying the theories to concrete pericopes, the reader can see how each model functions and where its explanatory limits appear.

The Healing of the Paralytic (Mark 2:1–12 // Matthew 9:1–8 // Luke 5:17–26)

Mark's version of the healing of the paralytic is the most vivid. Jesus teaches in a crowded house in Capernaum. When the crowd blocks access, four men remove part of the roof and lower their friend into the room. Jesus forgives the man's sins, provoking accusations of blasphemy, then heals him before the astonished crowd (Mark 2:1–12). Matthew tells the same story more briefly. There is no mention of the house or roof, no crowd breaking through obstacles. Jesus simply heals the man, and the crowd glorifies God for granting such authority to human beings (Matt 9:1–8). Luke's version lies between the two. He includes the roof incident but adds that Pharisees and teachers of the law had gathered from all over Galilee and Judea (Luke 5:17–26).

Those who affirm Markan Priority see Mark's vividness as an indication of originality: Matthew abridges Mark's long narrative to highlight theology, while Luke expands and refines it. The Farrer Hypothesis agrees that Mark was first but proposes that Luke also read Matthew, borrowing and reshaping elements from both earlier accounts. Scholars working within the Griesbach tradition reverse this direction: Matthew came first, Luke elaborated the story, and Mark later blended their versions into a concise narrative. The Augustinian model, following ancient testimony, maintains that Matthew wrote first, Mark summarized his Gospel, and Luke, writing third, drew on both predecessors.

Across these readings, the same episode reveals the hermeneutical character of each hypothesis. Some emphasize literary growth from Mark to Matthew and Luke; others see a process of abbreviation from fuller earlier sources. Each pattern of dependence produces a distinct theological and narrative interpretation.

The Temptation Narrative (Mark 1:12–13 // Matthew 4:1–11 // Luke 4:1–13)

Mark's description of Jesus' temptation is stark and compressed. The Spirit drives Jesus into the wilderness, where he is tempted by Satan and ministered to by angels (Mark 1:12–13). Matthew and Luke expand this terse summary into a fully developed dialogue between Jesus and the devil. Matthew's version unfolds in three temptations: the command to turn stones into bread, the challenge at the pinnacle of the temple, and the offer of the kingdoms of the world (Matt 4:1–11). Luke's account follows the same structure but places the temple scene last to bring the narrative to Jerusalem, a symbolic center in his Gospel (Luke 4:1–13).

For proponents of the Two-Source Theory, this expansion reflects a shared written source, Q, which contained a fuller version of the temptation story. Matthew preserved Q's order; Luke rearranged it for theological reasons. Advocates of the Farrer model reject Q and argue that Luke used Matthew directly, adapting the story's structure to his own emphasis on Jerusalem. The Griesbach Hypothesis views Matthew's threefold version as the earliest, Luke's as a deliberate rearrangement, and Mark's as a condensed summary of both. The Augustinian approach follows the same general sequence (i.e., Matthew first, Mark abridging, Luke harmonizing) but regards the order as shaped by theological intent rather than by a hypothetical source.

Here the case illustrates how each theory handles double tradition material. The Two-Source model accounts for Matthew and Luke's common expansion by positing Q, while Q-free alternatives attribute their similarity to direct literary contact.

The Beatitudes and the Sermon on the Mount/Plain (Matthew 5:1–12 // Luke 6:20–26)

In Matthew, Jesus ascends a mountain, sits to teach, and delivers nine beatitudes that emphasize inner virtue and righteousness: "Blessed are the poor in spirit, for theirs is the kingdom of heaven" (Matt 5:3). In Luke, Jesus stands on a level place and pronounces four blessings (on the poor, hungry, weeping, and persecuted) balanced by four woes (Luke 6:20–26).

For Two-Source advocates, this passage reflects independent use of Q by Matthew and Luke. Matthew expanded the blessings into a comprehensive sermon and spiritualized poverty into "poor in spirit," while Luke preserved the more literal form and added corresponding woes. Modern reconstructions of Q often treat Luke's version as closer to the earliest stratum of the tradition.

Supporters of the Farrer Hypothesis view Luke's sermon as a creative reworking of Matthew's. Luke condensed Matthew's nine beatitudes into four, paired them with woes, and shifted the focus from internal disposition to social reversal. For the Griesbach and Augustinian hypotheses, Matthew's version again stands first, Luke reshapes it for his Gentile audience, and Mark omits the sermon entirely.

This example shows how questions of sequence influence interpretation. Whether Luke abbreviated Matthew or both used Q affects how one perceives the theological contrast between the two Gospels: Luke's concern for the poor versus Matthew's emphasis on inner righteousness.

Peter's Confession and Passion Predictions (Mark 8:27–33 // Matthew 16:13–23 // Luke 9:18–22)

In Mark, Peter's confession serves as a turning point. Jesus asks, "Who do you say that I am?" and Peter responds, "You are the Messiah" (Mark 8:29). Immediately afterward, Jesus predicts his suffering and rebukes Peter's protest: "Get behind me, Satan" (8:33).

Matthew reproduces the scene but adds Jesus' blessing of Peter ("You are Peter, and on this rock I will build my church") and the promise of the keys of the kingdom (Matt 16:17–19). Luke omits both the blessing and the rebuke, offering a concise narrative in which Peter confesses and Jesus announces his passion (Luke 9:18–22).

For proponents of Markan Priority, the pattern is clear: Matthew expands Mark's brief narrative with material reflecting his ecclesial interests, while Luke refines the story by omitting potentially difficult details. Advocates of the Farrer Hypothesis interpret Luke's omissions as deliberate editing of Matthew's version to avoid an overemphasis on Peter's authority. The Griesbach and Augustinian models reverse the order, viewing Matthew's account as earliest and Mark's as a conflation or abbreviation that preserves the tension between Peter's insight and misunderstanding.

This episode highlights how each hypothesis addresses theological development. Markan Priority sees Matthew and Luke as redactors of Mark's raw narrative; Matthew's priority models view Mark as simplifying Matthew's mature theology.

The Transfiguration (Mark 9:2–8 // Matthew 17:1–8 // Luke 9:28–36)

Mark narrates the Transfiguration with characteristic immediacy: Jesus' clothes become dazzling white, Moses and Elijah appear, and a voice declares, "This is my Son, the Beloved; listen to him" (Mark 9:2–7).

Matthew follows Mark closely but intensifies the scene. Jesus' face shines "like the sun," and the disciples fall on their faces in reverence. The divine voice adds, "with him I am well pleased," echoing the baptism narrative (Matt 17:1–8). Luke again adapts the story in distinctive ways: he sets it during prayer, describes Jesus' appearance as changing, and reports that Moses and Elijah speak about his "departure" in Jerusalem (Luke 9:28–36).

According to the Two-Source Theory, Mark's account came first and was expanded by Matthew and Luke in different ways: Matthew emphasizing Jesus' majesty, Luke highlighting his coming passion. The Farrer Hypothesis attributes Luke's distinctive theological touches to his reading of both Mark and Matthew together. The Griesbach and Augustinian models continue to see Matthew's version as foundational, Luke's as an interpretive adaptation, and Mark's as a later synthesis of the two.

Each interpretation shows the same pattern: where one model sees development and redaction, another sees condensation and summary. The evidence remains open to multiple readings, depending on the assumed sequence of dependence.

Reflection on Method

These case studies demonstrate that no single passage can resolve the Synoptic Problem. Each hypothesis can account for the data in some way, but the more significant question is how well each model explains the *overall* pattern across many examples.

For defenders of Markan Priority and the Two-Source model, the argument lies in the cumulative convergence of evidence: Mark's shorter length, rougher style, distinctive order, and the tendency of Matthew and Luke to polish and expand his narratives. When these features appear repeatedly, they suggest that Mark's Gospel stands at the beginning of the written tradition.

Advocates of the Farrer Hypothesis emphasize a different kind of cumulative argument. They point to editorial fatigue, which are places where Luke begins revising Matthew but inadvertently reverts to Matthew's language or structure, and are highly diagnostic. For these interpreters, a few telling examples of fatigue reveal literary dependence more clearly than broad statistical trends.

Proponents of the Griesbach and Two-Gospel Hypothesis find their cumulative evidence in alternating primitivity. Across the double tradition, they note that sometimes Luke's version appears more primitive, sometimes Matthew's. This variation, they argue, makes more sense if Luke used Matthew than if both relied on a hypothetical Q.

Supporters of the Augustinian sequence appeal to historical memory rather than textual reconstruction. The consistent testimony of early Christian writers that Matthew wrote first, followed by Mark and then Luke, forms its own kind of cumulative evidence. For these interpreters, the reliability of ancient tradition and the theological harmony of the canonical order outweigh speculative reconstructions of lost documents.

In each case, what counts as "evidence" depends on one's methodological commitment, whether that commitment be textual, historical, or theological. Comparative study of pericopes reminds us that the Synoptic Problem cannot be settled by a single criterion but only by weighing diverse patterns that recur throughout the Gospels.

Conclusion

The Synoptic Problem is not solved by theory alone but by close attention to the texts themselves. Examining these five pericopes (the healing of the paralytic, the temptation narrative, the Beatitudes, Peter's confession, and the Transfiguration) shows how each hypothesis accounts for the same data in distinct ways.

The Two-Source model explains the double tradition by postulating a lost sayings source, though it requires accepting a document never discovered. The Farrer model removes Q entirely, portraying Luke as a creative interpreter of both Mark and Matthew, yet must explain Luke's freedom in rearranging his sources. The Griesbach and Augustinian approaches restore Matthew's priority and portray Mark as a later conflator or summarizer, but they must grapple with Mark's distinctive language and style.

No single pericope decides the matter. Each contributes one piece to a mosaic that remains incomplete. What emerges most clearly is not a definitive solution but an appreciation of the complexity and richness of the Synoptic tradition. The diversity of hypotheses reflects the layered and living nature of the Gospel witness itself, a tradition shaped by memory, faith, and literary creativity.

Figure 9.1. Evidence in Practice: Selected Pericope Comparisons

Pericope	Two-Source Theory	Farrer Hypothesis	Griesbach / Two-Gospel Hypo-thesis	Augustinian Hypothesis
Healing of the Paralytic (Mk 2:1–12 // Mt 9:1–8 // Lk 5:17–26)	Mark earliest; Matthew abbreviates; Luke expands	Mark earliest; Luke uses both Mark and Matthew	Matthew earliest; Luke expands; Mark conflates	Matthew earliest; Mark abbreviates; Luke synthesizes both
Temptation Narrative (Mk 1:12–13 // Mt 4:1–11 // Lk 4:1–13)	Q supplies three temptations; Matthew keeps order; Luke rearranges	Luke uses Matthew; reorders to climax in Jerusalem	Matthew earliest; Luke adapts; Mark abbrevi-ates	Matthew earliest; Mark abbreviates; Luke uses both
Beatitudes (Mt 5:1–12 // Lk 6:20–26)	Q source with blessings; Matthew expands to nine, Luke keeps four plus woes	Luke reworks Matthew; condenses and adds woes	Matthew earliest; Luke adapts socially; Mark omits	Matthew earliest; Mark omits; Luke blends both
Peter's Confession (Mk 8:27–33 // Mt 16:13–23 // Lk 9:18–22)	Mark earliest; Matthew expands; Luke omits awkward details	Luke knows Matthew; suppresses Peter's primacy	Matthew earliest; Luke abbrevi-ates; Mark conflates	Matthew earliest; Mark abbreviates; Luke synthesizes
Transfigur-ation (Mk 9:2–8 // Mt 17:1–8 // Lk 9:28–36)	Mark first; Matthew heightens majesty; Luke emphasizes passion	Luke adapts both Mark and Matthew; adds theology	Matthew earliest; Luke reworks; Mark conflates	Matthew earliest; Mark abbreviates; Luke integrates

Chapter 10
Case Studies

Expanding the Inquiry

The preceding chapter demonstrated how competing hypotheses can be tested by examining individual pericopes side by side. Those briefly worked examples illustrated how each theory interprets specific wording, order, and theology within short passages. In this chapter, the same analytical approach is applied to broader narrative units. These extended case studies, which are drawn from major scenes and discourses that shape the Synoptic story, allow the hypotheses to be tested across a wider canvas.

The selected examples represent varied literary types: passion narrative, discourse, parable, prophetic rejection, and infancy account. Together they reveal not only how the evangelists used their sources but also how theological and narrative patterns developed as the Gospels took written form.

The Passion Narrative (Mark 14–15 // Matthew 26–27 // Luke 22–23)

The passion story provides the most extensive and continuous material shared among the Synoptic Gospels. Nearly every event appears in all three: the Last Supper, arrest, trials, crucifixion, and burial. Verbal parallels often run word for word, while smaller differences disclose each evangelist's perspective.

In Mark, the passion unfolds with dramatic urgency. The narrative moves swiftly from the anointing at Bethany through the betrayal, trials, and crucifixion. Jesus is silent before his accusers; his disciples flee; and at the cross he cries, "My God, my God, why have you forsaken me?" (Mark 15:34).

Matthew closely follows Mark's structure but expands at key moments. He heightens the fulfillment of Scripture, adds the dream of Pilate's wife, introduces the episode of Judas's remorse, and records cosmic signs at the death of Jesus. His Gospel ends with an earthquake and the confession of the centurion, "Truly this was the Son of God!" (Matt 27:54).

Luke again follows the general outline but shapes the narrative differently. Jesus prays for his executioners, comforts the women of Jerusalem, promises paradise to the repentant thief, and dies in trust: "Father, into your hands I commend my spirit" (Luke 23:46). Luke's version softens the note of abandonment that dominates Mark.

The Two-Source Theory explains these relationships by seeing Mark as the primary narrative source that Matthew and Luke adapted independently. The Farrer Hypothesis agrees on Markan priority but holds that Luke also knew Matthew, accounting for shared expansions such as Pilate's emphasis and the centurion's confession. In Griesbach and Augustinian models, Matthew's longer version stands first, Luke modifies it, and Mark later condenses and combines.

The passion narrative thus confirms that the evangelists inherited a common story yet reinterpreted it for their communities. Whether one begins with Mark or Matthew, the later writers express distinct theological emphases: fulfillment for Matthew, compassion for Luke. Such emphases indicate that the tradition was both stable and adaptable.

The Mission Discourse and Sending of the Twelve (Mark 6:7–13 // Matthew 10:1–42 // Luke 9:1–6; 10:1–20)

All three Synoptics describe Jesus commissioning his followers for mission, yet the scope and tone differ markedly.

Mark gives a brief, practical summary: the Twelve are sent two by two with minimal provisions to preach and heal. They are to stay where welcomed and shake the dust from their feet where rejected (Mark 6:7–13).

Matthew transforms this simple sending into an extended discourse (Matt 10:1–42). The instructions become a charter for apostolic mission: warnings of persecution, promises of the Spirit's aid, and sayings about confession, family division, and discipleship. Matthew places the discourse early, presenting Jesus as a new Moses giving authoritative teaching.

Luke divides the material into two missions: first the Twelve (9:1–6), then seventy-two others (10:1–20). His additions, including parallels to Old

Testament prophetic patterns and the vision of Satan's fall, connect the mission to salvation's cosmic scope.

The Two-Source model attributes Matthew and Luke's fuller material to Q, a sayings source containing missionary instructions. Farrer interprets Luke's double mission as creative reuse of Matthew's discourse, expanded to include a wider circle of disciples. Griesbach and Augustinian readings reverse the sequence: Matthew's discourse comes first, Luke reshapes it into narrative form, and Mark shortens it into a simple report.

Across models, this comparison shows how a brief commission could evolve into a theological manifesto for mission. The form of Jesus' charge reflects the developing identity of the church itself.

The Parable of the Talents / Pounds (Matthew 25:14–30 // Luke 19:11–27)

This parable, often cited in discussions of redaction, illustrates how similar material can be profoundly reinterpreted.

Matthew's version occurs within the eschatological discourse and emphasizes accountability: three servants receive talents; two invest wisely; one hides his money and is condemned. The moral concerns readiness for the master's return and faithful stewardship.

Luke places a comparable story earlier, near the triumphal entry. Here ten servants receive one mina each; one gains ten, another five, a third none. The parable concludes with the master's severe judgment and his rejection of opponents. Luke's additions, such as the nobleman's journey to receive a kingdom, suggest political allegory and foreshadow the rejection of Jesus.

For Two-Source interpreters, the differences reflect independent adaptation of a parable circulating in oral form. The Farrer Hypothesis views Luke as reworking Matthew's text, transforming a moral lesson into an eschatological drama tied to his Jerusalem theme. Griesbach and Augustinian proponents again take Matthew as the source, Luke as the adapter, and Mark as omitting the story.

Whatever the sequence, both versions reveal the evangelists' artistry. They transmit a shared parabolic tradition while reshaping it to address different communities: Matthew urging diligence in discipleship, Luke warning of accountability and rejected kingship.

The Rejection at Nazareth (Mark 6:1–6 // Matthew 13:53–58 // Luke 4:16–30)

The rejection scene exposes how narrative placement can alter meaning.

In Mark, the episode comes midway through the ministry. Jesus teaches in his hometown synagogue, meets skepticism, and marvels at their unbelief. The story functions as a transition between Galilean ministry and mission of the Twelve.

Matthew reproduces the account with minor stylistic improvement but omits Mark's astonishment. The episode still precedes the mission discourse and signals widening opposition.

Luke relocates the story to the opening of Jesus' ministry (Luke 4:16–30). Expanding it into a major programmatic scene, he includes a reading from Isaiah 61, a sermon on God's mercy to outsiders, and the violent reaction of the townspeople. What is a local rejection in Mark becomes, for Luke, a preview of universal mission and prophetic suffering.

Markan priority explains Luke's and Matthew's versions as theological rearrangements of Mark's simpler narrative. The Farrer model attributes Luke's innovations partly to his reading of Matthew, transforming Matthew's summary into a dramatic inauguration of Jesus' mission. Griesbach and Augustinian readings again reverse direction: Matthew's account earliest, Luke elaborating, Mark abbreviating.

The Nazareth episode demonstrates that redaction is not merely editorial but interpretive. By relocating or expanding tradition, each evangelist announces the character of Jesus' mission.

The Infancy Narratives (Matthew 1–2 // Luke 1–2)

The birth stories, absent from Mark, provide the clearest evidence of independent composition.

Matthew's infancy narrative centers on Joseph. Dreams guide his decisions; quotations from Scripture punctuate the story; Gentile magi honor the child while Herod plots his death. The narrative foreshadows Jesus as the fulfillment of Israel's history and the true son called out of Egypt.

Luke's narrative centers on Mary. It opens with parallel announcements to Zechariah and Mary, continues through songs of praise (the Magnificat, Benedictus, and Nunc Dimittis) and culminates in the presentation at the temple and the boy Jesus among the teachers. The tone is liturgical and universal, presenting salvation for all peoples.

Since Mark contains no infancy story, the Two-Source Theory sees these narratives as independent creations of Matthew and Luke. The Farrer Hypothesis proposes that Luke knew Matthew's version but recast it with new characters and theology. The Griesbach and Augustinian models retain Matthean priority: Matthew wrote first, Luke expanded, and Mark began his Gospel later without birth material.

Regardless of order, both evangelists wrote theology through narrative. The birth stories proclaim from the outset what their Gospels will later demonstrate: Jesus is Messiah and Savior, rooted in Israel's story yet destined for the world.

Looking Ahead
From Analysis to Reflection

These broader case studies confirm what the shorter examples of Chapter 9 first revealed: each Synoptic hypothesis can explain the data in some measure, yet none alone captures the full complexity of the Gospel tradition. When analyzed across extended narratives (the Passion, the Mission, the Parables, the Nazareth episode, and the Infancy stories), the same patterns reappear: shared structure, distinctive voice, and theological purpose.

Figure 10.1. Case Studies in Synoptic Comparison

Case Study	**Two-Source Theory**	**Farrer Hypothesis**	**Gries-bach Hypo-thesis**	**Augustinian Hypothesis**
Passion Narrative (Mk 14–15 // Mt 26–27 // Lk 22–23)	Mark earliest; Matthew expands with fulfillment; Luke adapts with special traditions	Mark earliest; Luke uses Matthew as well, explaining minor agreements	Matthew earliest; Luke adapts; Mark conflates Matthew and Luke	Matthew earliest; Mark abbreviates; Luke integrates both
Mission Discourse (Mk 6:7–13 // Mt 10:1–42 // Lk 9:1–6; 10:1–20)	Mark core; Matthew expands via Q; Luke uses Mark + Q with seventy mission	Luke uses both Mark and Matthew; condenses discourse and creates seventy mission	Matthew earliest; Luke abbreviat es and reorganiz es; Mark condense s	Matthew earliest; Mark abbreviates; Luke synthesizes Matthew and Mark
Parable of the Talents/ Pounds (Mt 25:14–30 // Lk 19:11–27)	Shared Q parable with divergent redaction (Matthew: proportion-al; Luke: equal opportun-ity)	Luke adapts Matthew; editorial fatigue explains inconsist-encies	Matthew earliest; Luke reworks Matthew; Mark omits	Matthew earliest; Mark omits; Luke draws on both
Rejection at Nazareth (Mk 6:1–6	Mark earliest; Matthew	Luke knows Mark and Matthew;	Matthew earliest; Luke	Matthew earliest; Mark abbreviates;

// Mt 13:53–58 // Lk 4:16–30)	follows closely; Luke relocates and expands with Isaianic sermon	relocates to start; adds Isaianic theme	expands; Mark abbreviates	Luke synthesizes both
Infancy Narratives (Mt 1–2 // Lk 1–2)	Independent special sources (M, L); Mark has none	Special traditions; Luke reshapes Matthew's account with new emphases	Matthew earliest; Luke reworks; Mark omits	Matthew earliest; Mark omits; Luke integrates both

The next stage of inquiry therefore moves beyond comparison toward interpretation and evaluation. Part IV will consider what these literary relationships mean for reading, theology, and faith. Having explored how the Gospels may have been composed, we now ask what their composition reveals about the nature of the Gospel itself.

Part IV
Implications and Horizons

Chapter 11
Consequences for Exegesis and Theology

Introduction
From Literary Analysis to Theological Insight

Having explored the Synoptic relationships and tested the hypotheses through case studies, we now move beyond literary analysis to theological interpretation. Source criticism has illuminated how the evangelists used and adapted their sources; it has shown that the Gospels are both historical and theological documents, which are crafted narratives that reveal faith through form. This chapter examines the implications of these discoveries for exegesis and theology. It considers how historical and literary findings shape our understanding of inspiration, revelation, authority, and the unity and diversity of the Gospel witness.

The study of sources, when viewed theologically, becomes a study of divine communication through human agency. Each evangelist received inherited tradition and interpreted it afresh for a new context. Recognizing this process invites a deeper appreciation of revelation as dynamic and participatory rather than static and mechanical.

The Nature of Gospel Composition and Inspiration

Source criticism reveals that inspiration operates within history, not outside it. The evangelists were not passive recorders of dictation but active theologians. Their creative use of sources (Mark's vivid immediacy, Matthew's structured teaching, and Luke's narrative polish) demonstrates that divine truth was expressed through human imagination, memory, and community reflection.

In this light, inspiration encompasses the entire process by which the Gospel tradition was transmitted, remembered, and reinterpreted. The Spirit worked not only in the initial events of Jesus' life but also in their retelling. The theological message of the Gospels, therefore, resides in the interplay of memory and faith: in the inspired re-presentation of Christ through distinct narrative forms.

This understanding reframes debates about biblical authority. To say that the Gospels are inspired is to affirm that their diversity belongs to revelation itself. The Spirit did not impose uniformity but cultivated coherence amid variety. The fourfold Gospel canon thus becomes a theological statement: truth is encountered in complementary perspectives rather than in a single univocal account.

Diversity and Unity in Revelation

The Synoptic Gospels embody a unity that is theological rather than verbal. Each evangelist tells the same story differently because each writes from within a specific community, for particular readers, and with distinct theological aims. This diversity of presentation is not an obstacle to faith but a means of grasping the richness of God's revelation.

Mark emphasizes the suffering Son of Man, revealing discipleship as costly obedience. Matthew portrays Jesus as teacher and new Moses, interpreting the law's fulfillment. Luke presents Christ as Savior of all, announcing the universal scope of salvation. These perspectives complement rather than contradict each other.

The plurality of the Gospel witness reveals divine wisdom expressed through human difference. Revelation unfolds not through repetition but through dialogue. The canon's unity, therefore, lies in its capacity to hold diversity in tension. What emerges is a theological symphony rather than a unison melody. The harmony of the Gospels models the unity of the Church itself, which confesses one faith through many voices.

Historical Jesus and Kerygmatic Christ

The distinction between the historical Jesus and the proclaimed Christ, which has been long debated in theology, takes new shape in light of Synoptic study. The evangelists did not invent the Christ of faith apart from the Jesus of history; rather, they interpreted the historical Jesus through the lens of resurrection faith. Their redactional activity shows how memory and proclamation are intertwined.

The Gospels' differences in detail or emphasis reflect the early Church's effort to articulate the meaning of Jesus' life and death for new contexts. The sayings, parables, and miracles were not transcribed verbatim but interpreted through preaching, worship, and catechesis. This process does not obscure truth but reveals it: the risen Lord encountered in faith is the same Jesus of Nazareth remembered in story.

Modern historical study, therefore, complements rather than competes with theology. To trace the evolution of tradition from oral proclamation to written Gospel is to witness the incarnation of revelation within human language and culture. The Christ who speaks through Scripture is both the Jesus of history and the Lord of faith.

Scripture, Authority, and Canon

The diversity of the Synoptic tradition inevitably raises questions of authority. How can Scripture be authoritative if its accounts differ? The answer lies in understanding authority not as uniform control but as faithful witness. The evangelists' freedom in shaping tradition reflects confidence that truth transcends any single formulation.

The canonization of four distinct Gospels affirms that authority in Scripture is relational and dialogical. Each Gospel authenticates and interprets the others. The canon's very structure invites readers into conversation, teaching that divine revelation is not exhausted by one voice.

For theology, this has far-reaching implications. It means that the authority of the Gospels is inseparable from their diversity. The Spirit who inspired the evangelists also guided the Church in recognizing the fourfold witness as normative. Canon and inspiration are thus two aspects of one mystery: the Word of God spoken through many witnesses, unified by the same Spirit.

Exegesis and the Life of the Church

Understanding the Gospels' literary relationships transforms both scholarly exegesis and ecclesial interpretation. Critical study, when practiced in faith, becomes a means of discipleship. To see how Matthew reshaped Mark or how Luke structured his Gospel is to glimpse the living tradition of interpretation within the Church itself.

For pastors and teachers, this means that textual comparison is not a threat to faith but a resource for proclamation. It teaches humility in interpretation, reminding readers that no single perspective captures the whole truth. It also encourages creative engagement, inviting preachers and readers to enter the same interpretive process the evangelists themselves embodied.

This insight has renewed importance in pastoral and theological contexts, particularly in global and digital environments. Diverse cultures encounter the Gospel in different ways, much as the early communities did. The Synoptic principle of unity through diversity models how the Gospel continues to take root across languages, cultures, and historical situations.

Theological Synthesis: Revelation through Human Mediation

The theology that emerges from Synoptic study affirms that revelation occurs through human mediation. The evangelists, like the prophets before them, were inspired interpreters. Their writings reveal that divine truth engages human creativity.

This view deepens the doctrine of inspiration by expanding it beyond the moment of dictation to encompass the whole life of the community. The same Spirit who inspired the events of Jesus' ministry also inspired their recollection, transmission, and literary expression.

Thus, the Synoptic Gospels offer a theology of revelation in narrative form. God speaks through story, memory, and interpretation. The divine Word becomes incarnate not only in flesh but also in text, shaped by the faith of those who bear witness. This incarnational understanding of Scripture bridges the divide between historical criticism and theology: the more deeply we study the human texture of the text, the more clearly we perceive its divine origin.

Hermeneutical Implications

Modern interpretation inherits this complex legacy. The task of exegesis is no longer to extract a single "original" meaning but to engage the dialogue between texts, traditions, and readers.

Synoptic comparison models this hermeneutic of dialogue. By setting the Gospels side by side, interpreters learn to hold difference and coherence in creative tension.

This approach challenges both fundamentalism, which fears diversity, and skepticism, which denies coherence. It invites a mature faith that trusts the Spirit to speak through complexity. The Synoptic Problem, viewed theologically, becomes a paradigm for reading Scripture as conversation rather than code.

In practice, this means that interpretation must be communal and historical. No reader stands outside tradition; every act of interpretation participates in the Church's ongoing reception of the Gospel. Critical methods thus serve the life of faith when they are integrated with worship, prayer, and communal discernment.

Conclusion

From Source Criticism to Theological Renewal

The study of the Synoptic Problem has moved from the search for a literary solution to a broader appreciation of the Gospel as theological witness. Each hypothesis (Two-Source, Farrer, Griesbach, or Augustinian) illuminates part of the mystery of revelation, showing how divine truth takes form through human retelling.

For modern readers, the implications are both scholarly and spiritual. Historical study enriches theological understanding; critical inquiry strengthens faith. The diversity of the Gospels, once seen as a problem, now appears as a gift. Such diversity is the means by which the Spirit communicates a fuller truth than any single account could convey.

As we move to the next chapter, attention will turn to contemporary questions. Chapter 12 explores how recent developments, including digital tools, global perspectives, and new hermeneutical approaches, extend and challenge traditional study of the Synoptic Gospels. The conversation continues, as it has from the beginning: faith seeking understanding through the living word of Scripture.

Chapter 12
Digital and Contemporary Horizons

Introduction
The Continuing Conversation

The study of the Synoptic Gospels never stands still. Each generation inherits the questions of the last and asks them anew. The classical disciplines, notably source, form, and redaction criticism, have not vanished. They continue to provide the grammar and structure within which newer approaches take shape. What has changed is the breadth of the conversation. Gospel scholarship now speaks with voices drawn from many cultures and disciplines, informed by advances in literary theory, social sciences, theology, and digital technology.

This chapter surveys these horizons and argues that source criticism remains central to them all. It is not a discarded method but the foundation that supports the architecture of contemporary Gospel interpretation.

From Source to Redaction to Narrative

Form and redaction criticism were natural extensions of the source-critical impulse. Where source criticism traced dependence among written texts, form criticism examined the oral traditions behind them, and redaction criticism analyzed the theological purposes of the evangelists. These stages demonstrate continuity, not replacement. Each depends upon recognizing literary relationships first revealed by source study.

Narrative criticism, emerging in the latter twentieth century, likewise presupposes this groundwork. The artistry of Mark's fast-paced story, Matthew's structured discourse, and Luke's expansive narrative becomes meaningful precisely because we can see how each evangelist adapted earlier material. Source criticism shows what was inherited; narrative criticism shows how it was reshaped into theology through story.

The same is true of rhetorical and reader-response approaches. The evangelists are not stenographers but persuasive authors who shape their audiences' imagination. Awareness of textual dependence enhances, rather than hinders, appreciation of their rhetorical craft.

Contextual and Constructive Theologies

The rise of contextual theologies (feminist, womanist, liberationist, postcolonial, and others) has changed the landscape of biblical interpretation. These movements arose as correctives to the historical biases of earlier scholarship, bringing to the foreground the perspectives of those marginalized by gender, race, or empire. Yet their insights intersect fruitfully with source criticism, not in opposition to it.

Feminist and womanist readings attend to the experiences and voices of women in the Gospels and in the interpretive community. They challenge patriarchal assumptions that shaped both ancient and modern readings. Source criticism assists this work by clarifying how the evangelists themselves treated traditions about women. For instance, comparing Mark's and Matthew's portrayals of the woman who anoints Jesus shows how theological emphasis and social assumption interact. Redactional differences reveal patterns of inclusion and omission that illuminate the role of women in early Christian memory.

Liberationist interpretations, arising significantly from Latin American, African, and Asian contexts, approach the Gospels through the lens of social justice and the struggle for freedom. They see in Jesus' proclamation of the kingdom a call to transform oppressive structures. Source criticism aids such readings by identifying how each evangelist emphasizes economic and political themes: Luke's concern for the poor, Matthew's attention to righteousness, Mark's critique of power. The comparative method provides the historical grounding that allows theology to engage concrete realities of injustice.

Postcolonial criticism examines the interaction between the Gospels and imperial power. The Roman world forms the backdrop of Jesus' ministry and the evangelists' writing; modern empires shape how readers perceive them. By distinguishing the voices of different evangelists, source criticism helps postcolonial interpreters hear both resistance and accommodation within the texts. The method that once traced literary dependence now enables discernment of ideological complexity.

In all these approaches, the task is not to abandon critical history but to enlarge it. This task brings social and theological imagination to bear upon the same textual relationships that early scholars first charted.

Social-Scientific and Cultural Readings

Anthropological and sociological perspectives analyze the cultural values that structure the Gospels. Honor and shame, patronage, purity, and kinship provide the social grammar of the ancient Mediterranean world. Studies by Bruce Malina, Jerome Neyrey, and John H. Elliott, among others, have shown how the evangelists address these realities. Yet once again, such insights depend on careful attention to literary relationships. Knowing which evangelist introduced or altered a saying reveals how social values were interpreted within specific communities.

Cultural readings broaden the conversation further. African interpreters explore communal and oral dimensions of the Gospel story; Asian scholars read Jesus in conversation with wisdom traditions; indigenous theologians highlight ecological and relational aspects of the text. Source criticism gives these readings a common foundation, allowing diverse perspectives to engage shared textual ground.

Memory, Orality, and the Living Tradition

Recent scholarship on memory and orality reframes the entire discussion of Gospel origins.

Werner Kelber and James D. G. Dunn describe how collective memory and oral performance shaped early Christian storytelling. Richard Bauckham emphasizes the role of eyewitness testimony. These studies reveal that the evangelists wrote within a living tradition of recollection and retelling.

Source criticism contributes by mapping the literary crystallization of this process. It shows how the oral tradition took specific written form in each Gospel. The tension between memory and redaction becomes a dialogue between fluid tradition and fixed text. In this sense, the classical methods and the newer memory approaches illuminate each other: both explore how faith remembers.

Canonical and Theological Reading

Canonical and theological interpretation of Scripture has revived interest in the final form of the text. Brevard Childs, Francis Watson, and Richard Hays argue that the Gospels must be read within the context of the Church's faith and the larger biblical canon. The purpose of criticism, in this view, is not to divide but to understand unity-in-diversity.

Here again, source criticism provides indispensable service. Recognizing how Matthew and Luke expand Mark or how Luke reorders material clarifies how theology develops through composition. Historical inquiry grounds theological reading in the concrete processes of inspiration. Without that grounding, theology risks abstraction. When joined together, history and faith reinforce one another: criticism becomes contemplation.

The Digital Turn

The twenty-first century has introduced a new frontier for Gospel study: the digital humanities. The comparative impulse that once produced printed synopses now finds expression in databases and algorithms.

Digital tools. Software such as *Accordance, Logos Bible Software,* and *BibleWorks* align Greek and vernacular texts, tag morphology, and generate instant concordances. Open-access programs like *STEPBible* and *Paratext* empower translation and textual comparison in multiple languages. Analytical tools such as *CollateX, Juxta,* and *Voyant Tools* conduct stylometric and lexical analysis, visualizing relationships between texts in charts and networks.

Pedagogical impact. In classrooms and online platforms, students can now place the Synoptic parallels side by side, trace verbal agreements, and identify redactional patterns in real time. What once took months of collation can now be accomplished in minutes, freeing interpreters to focus on meaning rather than mechanics.

Global access. Digital resources democratize scholarship. Theologians and students in the Global South can access the same texts and tools once confined to research libraries in Europe and North America. This aligns perfectly with the mission of digital theological initiatives worldwide, bringing critical study into conversation with pastoral and contextual needs.

Technology does not replace interpretation; it expands the circle of interpreters. The digital turn represents the newest chapter in the long history of comparison that began with the earliest synopses of the Gospels. Source criticism finds fresh life in electronic form.

Globalization and Dialogue

Globalization has transformed Gospel study from a largely Euro-Atlantic conversation into a genuinely worldwide dialogue. Across Africa, Asia, Latin America, and Oceania, scholars read the Synoptic Gospels within living traditions of orality, communal ethics, and interreligious encounter. These contexts do not merely "apply" exegesis after the fact; they generate interpretive questions at the level of method. Concerns about land and ecology, migration and diaspora, caste and ethnicity, and the legacy of empire all shape how readers approach Matthew, Mark, and Luke. When source criticism identifies how a pericope circulates or changes from one evangelist to another, global interpreters ask how those textual dynamics illuminate the movement of the Gospel across cultures. They ask how memory, authority, and community negotiate continuity and change.

The digital turn amplifies this global conversation but also exposes asymmetries. Online corpora, morphologically tagged texts, and alignment tools are increasingly available to readers who once lacked access to major libraries.

Mobile-first platforms, offline packages, and low-bandwidth resources now place synoptic comparison into classrooms from Kampala to Kolkata. At the same time, global participation raises questions about language hegemony and data colonialism: whose Greek text, whose English glosses, whose metadata and tagging conventions set the frame within which others must work? Source criticism can model a more equitable practice by encouraging locally led research questions, shared datasets, and co-authorship that recognizes the intellectual labor of scholars outside the global North. The method's comparative habits, including patient description, transparency of evidence, and careful attribution, have become ethical habits for collaboration.

Global dialogue also reshapes pedagogy. In communities where communal storytelling and song remain central, synoptic comparison is naturally performed aloud: students hear how Matthew, Mark, and Luke phrase the same saying with different emphases, and they connect those editorial choices to their own practices of testimony and liturgy. Digital synopses projected in a classroom or shared on a phone enable side-by-side reading in local languages, fostering bilingual or trilingual exegesis that respects linguistic nuance. Translation projects draw on Paratext and similar tools to test renderings against parallels, helping teams decide when uniformity serves clarity and when distinct wordings better carry each evangelist's theology. In this sense, globalization is not merely about distributing Western tools more widely; it is about letting new communities teach all readers how the Gospels sound when voiced in different tongues.

Intercultural reading further invites South-to-South exchange. African womanist readings of Luke's birth narratives speak fruitfully with Latin American liberation readings of Luke-Acts; Asian postcolonial interpretations of Mark's passion engage Pacific Islander reflections on empire and resilience. Source criticism serves these encounters by providing a shared textual map (including agreement, divergence, order, and redaction) on which differing theological insights can be located without being flattened. The same synoptic grid that once adjudicated hypotheses becomes a table around which communities bring their histories, sufferings, and hopes to bear on the text. In this way, globalization does not relativize Scripture; it multiplies concrete points of contact where the one Gospel is heard through many voices.

Finally, a global perspective reframes reception. The Synoptic Gospels have always traveled, first within the Mediterranean, then along paths of trade, mission, and migration. Today's diasporas create new "synoptic" spaces in which diverse traditions share neighborhoods and parishes. Pastors and teachers draw on narrative criticism to preach coherent Gospel arcs, on social-scientific insights to name shame and honor in immigrant experience, and on source-critical awareness to respect each evangelist's voice in multilingual congregations. The measure of faithful globalization is not agreement imposed from the center but mutual recognition: a discipline that listens across boundaries, returns credit where it is due, and learns to see in difference the generosity of the canonical fourfold witness.

A Living Discipline

Contemporary Gospel studies are wide-ranging and interdisciplinary, yet the comparative instincts of source criticism continue to hold the conversation together. The discipline's patient work, which observes verbal agreement, tracking order, weighing redaction, has become more, not less, valuable as interpreters engage narrative artistry, social location, feminist and womanist critique, postcolonial analysis, and digital methods. By clarifying what each evangelist inherited and how he reshaped it, source criticism supplies the historical and literary coordinates within which constructive readings can proceed responsibly. In a global classroom, it offers a shared grammar that enables dialogue across languages and traditions while protecting the particularity of each Gospel's theological voice.

At the same time, the discipline itself is renewed by that dialogue. Global readers ask questions the older guild did not ask; feminist and liberationist interpreters expose assumptions long taken for granted; digital tools reveal patterns otherwise invisible to the eye. The result is not a displacement of classical methods but their re-centering within a larger ecology of interpretation, one that is collaborative, ethically alert, and open to the Spirit's work in many contexts. When comparison serves communion, the synoptic enterprise becomes an act of reconciliation: different witnesses held together for the sake of the one Gospel they proclaim.

Looking ahead, the most promising work will be integrative. Scholars and students will move nimbly between textual alignment and narrative analysis, between social history and theological interpretation, between local concerns and global partnerships. Open data and shared platforms can lower barriers to participation; locally driven research agendas and co-authored projects can correct imbalances of power and credit. In such a future, source criticism remains what it has always been at its best: a living discipline, hospitable to new voices and new tools, devoted to reading Matthew, Mark, and Luke carefully enough that the Church may hear them, both separately and together, more truly.

Chapter 13
Reflection and Conclusion

The Journey and Its Meaning

This book has traced a long journey, from the first questions of literary dependence to the wide horizons of contemporary and digital interpretation. Along the way, we have rediscovered the vitality of the Synoptic tradition and the creativity of those who study it. What began as an analysis of textual relationships has unfolded into a meditation on revelation itself. The relationships among Matthew, Mark, and Luke are more than puzzles of dependence; they are windows into the way divine truth inhabits human story.

The Synoptic Gospels remind us that revelation is historical, dialogical, and communal. The Word becomes flesh not only in the life of Jesus but in the lives of those who remember, interpret, and proclaim him. The patterns of dependence that source criticism uncovers are the literary traces of this theological truth: faith is transmitted through relationship. The same comparative spirit that seeks to understand how one Gospel influenced another teaches us to value difference as a site of divine communication.

The Fourfold Gospel and the Nature of Revelation

The Church's decision to preserve four Gospels rather than harmonize them into one was itself a theological act. The early Christians recognized that the fullness of the Gospel could not be contained in a single telling. Each evangelist gives voice to a different facet of the same mystery. Mark's raw immediacy, Matthew's didactic precision, and Luke's narrative grace all together reveal a Christ who transcends every attempt at reduction.

Modern scholarship, by clarifying the relationships among these texts, confirms this ancient intuition. The more closely we compare the Gospels, the more we perceive the unity that resides within their diversity. Comparison does not erode faith; it displays its complexity. The fourfold Gospel stands as a model for Christian thought itself: one truth articulated through multiple perspectives. It teaches that divine revelation welcomes difference and that the quest for harmony must never suppress distinct voices.

In an age of fragmentation and polarization, the canonical decision for plurality carries renewed significance. The Gospels invite not uniformity but communion. They show that coherence arises not from enforced sameness but from shared witness to Christ. The fourfold Gospel is, in this sense, both a theological symbol and an ethical imperative: truth is relational, and faith is sustained through conversation.

The Interpreter's Vocation

To study the Gospels is to join the company of interpreters who have sought, across centuries, to hear again the living voice of Christ. The interpreter's work is not merely analytical; it is vocational. Every careful reading, every footnote and translation, participates in the same interpretive task begun by the evangelists themselves.

In the modern world, that vocation has acquired new dimensions. Digital access has democratized biblical study, opening archives once limited to a few. Theologians in Nairobi or Seoul now compare manuscripts and commentaries once housed only in European libraries. Yet this accessibility brings responsibility. Scholarship in the digital age must resist the temptation of speed without depth and technology without wisdom. The tools of computation must serve the discipline of contemplation.

The vocation of Gospel study also calls for collaboration across global boundaries. In an interconnected world, the work of interpretation is no longer confined to any single culture or language. African theologians, Asian readers, Latin American liberationists, and Western historical critics all contribute to a conversation that mirrors the polyphony of the Gospels themselves. The task of the modern reader and interpreter is not only to speak but to listen and to practice the humility that allows truth to emerge through dialogue.

When pursued in this spirit, Gospel scholarship becomes an act of communion. It links universities, seminaries, and local congregations in a shared pursuit of understanding. The ultimate goal is not mastery of the text but participation in the mystery it reveals.

Theology after Criticism

Critical study and theological reflection are sometimes imagined as adversaries, but the history of Gospel interpretation shows that they are partners. Source criticism, redaction analysis, and narrative reading do not undermine theology; they make theology possible. To discern how Matthew or Luke reinterprets Mark is to witness inspiration at work. It is to see how divine truth unfolds through human creativity.

Theology after criticism acknowledges that revelation is not given all at once but emerges through process and conversation. The Gospels teach us that God's Word does not bypass culture or language but inhabits them. Each evangelist's redactional choices bear the marks of context, faith, and imagination. The same Spirit who inspired Jesus' words inspired the memory of them, the writing of them, and the reading of them.

For contemporary theology, this means that historical precision and spiritual devotion belong together. Faith without critical awareness risks sentimentality; criticism without faith risks sterility. The healthiest scholarship integrates both the head that analyzes and the heart that worships. In this integration, study becomes praise.

Future Directions in Gospel Studies

The study of the Synoptic Gospels will continue to evolve. New tools and new questions will open fresh paths of exploration. Several directions already beckon.

First, the digital humanities will deepen textual and linguistic analysis. Artificial intelligence, corpus linguistics, and advanced alignment software will allow scholars to visualize relationships and stylistic tendencies that were once invisible. These technologies will not end interpretation but refine it, freeing readers to focus on theological and ethical questions that transcend the mechanics of data.

Second, memory and trauma studies invite renewed attention to how suffering shapes narrative. The passion stories, in particular, speak to communities that remember persecution and loss. Reading them through the lens of collective trauma connects ancient experiences of violence with modern contexts of displacement and oppression.

Third, ecological and creation-focused readings of the Gospels are emerging. The Synoptic portrayal of Jesus, which incorporates him teaching by the sea, praying on mountains, and calming storms, invites reflection on the relationship between the Creator and creation. Such readings situate redemption within the broader renewal of the earth, reminding readers that salvation is cosmic in scope.

Fourth, global and intercultural scholarship will continue to transform the field. The conversation among feminist, womanist, liberationist, and postcolonial interpreters will grow richer as their readings intersect with historical-critical and digital approaches. The future belongs to integrative methods, approaches that are simultaneously critical and constructive, historical and theological, contextual and canonical.

In all these developments, the Synoptic Gospels remain at the center. Their comparative texture, narrative coherence, and theological depth ensure that they will continue to shape Christian thought and imagination. The next generation of readers will not merely inherit this tradition; they will expand it, finding in the old questions new possibilities.

The Word That Keeps Speaking

The Synoptic Gospels end not with finality but with commission: with Jesus sending his followers into the world to proclaim what they have seen and heard. The same dynamic governs the study of these texts. Every discovery, every insight, propels the interpreter outward. Scholarship, like discipleship, is a journey without closure.

To read the Gospels synoptically is to participate in their theology. It is to recognize that truth is dialogical, that revelation unfolds through many witnesses. The comparative work of the scholar mirrors the reconciling work of the Spirit: bringing distinct voices into harmony without erasing their individuality. In this sense, the discipline itself becomes a parable of the Gospel it serves.

As we conclude, the invitation remains open. The evangelists have spoken, the generations of interpreters have responded, and the conversation continues. The fourfold Gospel, with its unity and diversity, stands as a symbol of hope for the Church and for scholarship alike. It teaches that difference need not divide, that truth can dwell in multiplicity, and that the Word of God, ever ancient and ever new, continues to speak through those who listen.

The Synoptic Problem, after all, was never merely a puzzle of sources. It is a testimony to revelation's abundance, which is the overflow of grace that requires more than one voice. To study it is to stand again where the Gospels themselves began: at the threshold of mystery, hearing the invitation to tell the story once more.

Bibliography

The following bibliography reflects the global and interdisciplinary character of contemporary Gospel scholarship. It includes classic and modern works foundational to the study of the Synoptic Gospels, together with contributions from women, scholars of color, and voices from Africa, Asia, Latin America, and Oceania. This broader representation honors the diversity of the worldwide Church and the growing recognition that biblical interpretation is a shared, collaborative endeavor across cultures, disciplines, and contexts.

Foundational Works in Synoptic Study

Augustine of Hippo. *De Consensu Evangelistarum.* Oxford: Clarendon Press, 1896.

Farmer, William R.. *The Synoptic Problem: A Critical Analysis.* Dillsboro, NC: Western North Carolina Press, 1964.

Goodacre, Mark. *The Case Against Q: Studies in Marcan Priority and the Synoptic Problem.* Harrisburg, PA: Trinity Press International, 2002.

Griesbach, J. J. *Synopsis Evangeliorum.* Halle: Hemmerde, 1776.

Holtzmann, Heinrich Julius. *Die synoptischen Evangelien: Ihr Ursprung und geschichtlicher Charakter.* Leipzig: Wilhelm Engelmann, 1863.

Streeter, B. H. *The Four Gospels: A Study of Origins.* London: Macmillan, 1924.

Weisse, Christian Hermann. *Die evangelische Geschichte, kritisch und philosophisch bearbeitet.* Leipzig: Breitkopf und Härtel, 1838.

Primary Bibliography

Aland, Kurt, and Barbara Aland. *The Text of the New Testament.* Grand Rapids: Eerdmans, 1987.

Bauckham, Richard. *Jesus and the Eyewitnesses: The Gospels as Eyewitness Testimony.* Grand Rapids: Eerdmans, 2006.

Bock, Darrell L. *Jesus According to Scripture: Restoring the Portrait from the Gospels.* Grand Rapids: Baker Academic, 2002.

Brown, Raymond E. *An Introduction to the New Testament.* New York: Doubleday, 1997.

Bultmann, Rudolf. *The History of the Synoptic Tradition.* Oxford: Basil Blackwell, 1963.

Childs, Brevard S. *The New Testament as Canon: An Introduction.* Philadelphia: Fortress Press, 1984.

Clivaz, Claire, David Hamidović, and Sarah Bowen Savant, eds. *Ancient Worlds in Digital Culture.* Leiden: Brill, 2016.

Culpepper, R. Alan. *Anatomy of the Fourth Gospel: A Study in Literary Design.* Philadelphia: Fortress Press, 1983.

Davies, W. D., and E. P. Sanders. *Studying the Synoptic Gospels.* London: SCM Press, 1989.

Dube, Musa W. *Postcolonial Feminist Interpretation of the Bible.* St. Louis: Chalice Press, 2000.

Dunn, James D. G. *Jesus Remembered.* Grand Rapids: Eerdmans, 2003.

Elliott, John H. *What Is Social-Scientific Criticism?* Minneapolis: Fortress Press, 1993.

Farmer, William R. *The Synoptic Problem.* Macon, GA: Mercer University Press, 1964.

Gaventa, Beverly Roberts. *Mary: Glimpses of the Mother of Jesus.* Columbia: University of South Carolina Press, 1995.

Goodacre, Mark. *Goulder and the Gospels: An Examination of a New Paradigm.* Sheffield: Sheffield Academic Press, 1996.

Goulder, Michael. *Luke: A New Paradigm.* Sheffield: JSOT Press, 1989.

Gutiérrez, Gustavo. *A Theology of Liberation.* Maryknoll, NY: Orbis Books, 1973.

Hays, Richard B. *Echoes of Scripture in the Gospels.* Waco, TX: Baylor University Press, 2016.

Holtzmann, Heinrich Julius. *Einleitung in das Neue Testament.* Freiburg: Mohr Siebeck, 1885.

Kelber, Werner H. *The Oral and the Written Gospel.* Philadelphia: Fortress Press, 1983.

Kingsbury, Jack Dean. *Matthew as Story.* Philadelphia: Fortress Press, 1986.

Kloppenborg, John S. *The Formation of Q: Trajectories in Ancient Wisdom Collections.* Philadelphia: Fortress Press, 1987.

Kloppenborg, John S. *Q: The Earliest Gospel.* Louisville, KY: Westminster John Knox Press, 2008.

Kwok, Pui-lan. *Postcolonial Imagination and Feminist Theology.* Louisville, KY: Westminster John Knox Press, 2005.

Liew, Tat-siong Benny. *What Is Asian American Biblical Hermeneutics? Reading the New Testament Discipleship Community.* Honolulu: University of Hawai'i Press, 2008.

Malina, Bruce J. *The New Testament World: Insights from Cultural Anthropology.* Louisville, KY: Westminster John Knox Press, 1981.

Manson, T. W. *The Sayings of Jesus.* London: SCM Press, 1949.

Meyer, Ben F. *The Aims of Jesus.* London: SCM Press, 1979.

Neyrey, Jerome H. *Honor and Shame in the Gospel of Matthew.* Louisville, KY: Westminster John Knox Press, 1998.

Oduyoye, Mercy Amba. *Introducing African Women's Theology.* Cleveland, OH: Pilgrim Press, 2001.

Parker, D. C. *An Introduction to the New Testament Manuscripts and Their Texts.* Cambridge: Cambridge University Press, 2008.

Peabody, David B., et al. *One Gospel from Two: Mark's Use of Matthew and Luke.* Harrisburg, PA: Trinity Press International, 2002.

Russell, Letty M. *Church in the Round: Feminist Interpretation in the Church.* Louisville, KY: Westminster John Knox Press, 1993.

Sanders, E. P. *The Tendencies of the Synoptic Tradition.* Cambridge: Cambridge University Press, 1969.

Schweitzer, Albert. *The Quest of the Historical Jesus.* London: Adam and Charles Black, 1910.

Stein, Robert H. *The Synoptic Problem: An Introduction.* Grand Rapids: Baker Book House, 1987.

Streeter, B. H. *The Four Gospels.* London: Macmillan, 1924.

Sugirtharajah, R. S. *Postcolonial Criticism and Biblical Interpretation.* Oxford: Oxford University Press, 2002.

Tamez, Elsa. *Bible of the Oppressed.* Maryknoll, NY: Orbis Books, 1982.

Ukpong, Justin S. *Reading the Bible in the Global Village: Contextual Hermeneutics.* Eugene, OR: Wipf and Stock, 2002.

Vatican II. *Dei Verbum (Dogmatic Constitution on Divine Revelation).* Vatican City: Libreria Editrice Vaticana, 1965.

Watson, Francis. *Gospel Writing: A Canonical Perspective.* Grand Rapids: Eerdmans, 2013.

Weems, Renita J. *Just a Sister Away: A Womanist Vision of Women's Relationships in the Bible.* San Diego: LuraMedia, 1988.

Wenham, John. *Redating Matthew, Mark and Luke: A Fresh Assault on the Synoptic Problem.* Downers Grove, IL: InterVarsity Press, 1992.

West, Gerald O. *Reading Other-wise: Socially Engaged Biblical Scholars Reading with Their Local Communities.* Atlanta: Society of Biblical Literature, 2007.

Wright, N. T. *Jesus and the Victory of God.* Minneapolis: Fortress Press, 1996.

Select Further Reading and Contemporary Studies

Boff, Leonardo. *Jesus Christ Liberator: A Critical Christology of Our Time.* Maryknoll, NY: Orbis Books, 1972.

Borg, Marcus J. *Meeting Jesus Again for the First Time.* San Francisco: HarperSanFrancisco, 1994.

Clivaz, Claire. *Ecritures digitales: Digital Writing, Digital Scriptures.* Geneva: Labor et Fides, 2019.

Dube, Musa W., and Jeffrey L. Staley, eds. *John and Postcolonialism: Travel, Space, and Power.* Sheffield: Sheffield Academic Press, 2002.

Gaventa, Beverly Roberts, and Richard B. Hays, eds. *Seeking the Identity of Jesus: A Pilgrimage.* Grand Rapids: Eerdmans, 2008.

Gutiérrez, Gustavo, and Gerhard Ludwig Müller. *On the Side of the Poor: The Theology of Liberation.* Maryknoll, NY: Orbis Books, 2015.

Maluleke, Tinyiko Sam. *Theology in Africa and the Africa in Theology.* Pretoria: University of South Africa Press, 2005.

Oduyoye, Mercy Amba, and Musimbi Kanyoro, eds. *The Will to Arise: Women, Tradition, and the Church in Africa.* Maryknoll, NY: Orbis Books, 1992.

Parker, D. C., and David G. Burke, eds. *Textual Scholarship and the Making of the New Testament.* Leiden: Brill, 2017.

Sugirtharajah, R. S., ed. *Voices from the Margin: Interpreting the Bible in the Third World.* Maryknoll, NY: Orbis Books, 1991.

Tamez, Elsa, and Pablo Richard, eds. *The Option for the Poor in the Bible and the Church.* Maryknoll, NY: Orbis Books, 1983.

Ukpong, Justin S. *Inculturation Hermeneutics: An African Approach to Biblical Interpretation.* Nairobi: Paulines Publications Africa, 1996.

West, Gerald O., and Musa W. Dube, eds. *The Bible in Africa: Transactions, Trajectories, and Trends.* Leiden: Brill, 2000.

Wright, N. T. *The Resurrection of the Son of God.* Minneapolis: Fortress Press, 2003.

Digital and Interdisciplinary Resources

Clivaz, Claire, Garrick V. Allen, and David Hamidović, eds. *Digital Humanities in Biblical, Early Jewish and Early Christian Studies.* Leiden: Brill, 2013.

Holmes, Michael W. *The Apostolic Fathers: Greek Texts and English Translations.* Grand Rapids: Baker Academic, 2007.

Parker, D. C. *Textual Scholarship and the Making of the New Testament.* Oxford: Oxford University Press, 2012.

Wasserman, Tommy, and Peter J. Gurry. *A New Approach to Textual Criticism: An Introduction to the Coherence-Based Genealogical Method.* Atlanta: Society of Biblical Literature, 2017.

Global and Contextual Hermeneutics

Dube, Musa W., Andrew Mbuvi, and Dora Mbuwayesango, eds. *Postcolonial Perspectives on African Biblical Interpretations*. Atlanta: Society of Biblical Literature, 2012.

Gutiérrez, Gustavo. *We Drink from Our Own Wells: The Spiritual Journey of a People*. Maryknoll, NY: Orbis Books, 1984.

Kwok, Pui-lan, and Elisabeth Schüssler Fiorenza, eds. *Christianity and Empire: Critical Studies in Christianity and Empire*. Harrisburg, PA: Trinity Press International, 2007.

Oduyoye, Mercy Amba. *Beads and Strands: Reflections of an African Woman on Christianity in Africa*. Maryknoll, NY: Orbis Books, 2004.

Russell, Letty M., Kwok Pui-lan, and Ada María Isasi-Díaz, eds. *Inheriting Our Mothers' Gardens: Feminist Theology in Third World Perspective*. Philadelphia: Westminster Press, 1988.

Weems, Renita J. *Battered Love: Marriage, Sex, and Violence in the Hebrew Prophets*. Minneapolis: Fortress Press, 1995.

West, Gerald O., ed. *The Stolen Bible: From Tool of Imperialism to African Icon*. Leiden: Brill, 2016.

www.ingramcontent.com/pod-product-compliance
Lightning Source LLC
LaVergne TN
LVHW012332100826
845148LV00017B/2128

* 9 7 9 8 8 9 7 3 1 2 8 8 7 *